SOCIAL CLASS,
LANGUAGE AND COMMUNICATION

PRIMARY SOCIALIZATION LANGUAGE AND EDUCATION

Edited by Basil Bernstein

University of London Institute of Education
Sociological Research Unit

I   Social Class, Language and Communication
Walter Brandis and Dorothy Henderson

II   A Linguistic Description and Computer Program
For Children's Speech
Geoffrey J. Turner and Bernard A. Mohan

III   Talk Reform
Dennis and Judy Gahagan

IV   A Question of Answers
W. P. Robinson and S. J. Rackstraw

Social Class Language and Communication

W. BRANDIS
and
D. HENDERSON

London
ROUTLEDGE & KEGAN PAUL

First published 1970
by Routledge & Kegan Paul Ltd
Broadway House, 68–74 Carter Lane
London E.C.4
Set I.B.M. by Academic Services Ltd
Printed in Great Britain
by Clarke, Doble & Brendon Ltd
I.S.B.N. 0 7100 6613 9

CONTENTS

Introduction

This monograph contains two linked research reports. The first, by Dorothy Henderson, explores the different effects of parental social class, the ability and sex of the child and a measure of the mother's reported communication to her child, upon aspects of five-year-old children's speech. In the second section of her report Mrs. Henderson shows the relationship between a measure of linguistic flexibility in children and their family's social class position. The second report is based upon some of the findings of the first interview with the mothers which took place in the summer before the children first went to school. The detailed report of this interview will be given in a future Sociological Research Unit monograph to be written by Jean Jones. In the report presented here, Bernstein and Brandis set out the construction and application of an index of maternal communication and control which is derived from the first questionnaire. Appendices to this report are by W. Brandis who undertook the statistical analysis of the data. These appendices are necessarily technical and are not intended for the lay reader.

It is appropriate here, in the first monograph, to recall the organising ability, drive and experimental grip of Dr. Peter Robinson who, between September 1965 and September 1966, was deputy head of the Sociological Research Unit. During that year a number of major projects were planned and analyses of data developed. Dr. Robinson played an important part in the shaping of these activities. He also drew up the factorial design which Mrs. Henderson used in the analysis of the children's speech. I should also like to express my gratitude to Rosalind Greenbaum, administrative secretary to the Sociological Research Unit, whose calmness, dedication and immense efficiency helped us through so many problems.

The work undertaken by the Sociological Research Unit will be reported in the following monographs to be published by Routledge and Kegan Paul. The order given here is not necessarily the order of their publication.

I am most grateful to the D.S.I.R. (now disbanded), the Nuffield Foundation, the Department of Education and Science and the Ford Foundation, for the grants which made this research possible, and even more to the two local Education Authorities who permitted the research to be carried out in the schools. I am also very much aware of my debt to Mr. Lionel Elvin, Director of the University of London Institute of Education, and to my colleagues for their support, advice and encouragement.

Basil Bernstein
Professor in the Sociology of Education
Head of the Sociological Research Unit
University of London Institute of Education.

THE HISTORY OF THE RESEARCH
Basil Bernstein

In this introduction to the first of the series of Sociological Research Unit Monographs, I shall give a general account of the work carried out over the last four years.

This research was initially planned whilst I was an honary research assistant to the Department of Phonetics, responsible to Professor D. Fry and Dr. F. Goldman-Eisler.* I received from both Professor Fry and Dr. Goldman-Eisler continuous advice, support and encouragement. The research developed out of a series of speculative papers which raised both general and particular questions about the inter-relationship between culture, social structure and orientations towards certain uses of language. The first research proposal was submitted to the Department of Education and Science (then the Ministry of Education) in 1962. As a result of a long series of discussions this first research proposal was dropped as the Department felt that it was too academic. The senior officials believed (and probably rightly) that any research in the area of language should include an exploratory attempt to develop a specific programme with teachers which might encourage children to explore various uses of language.

Five general areas of enquiry eventually crystallised:

1 A study of social class differences in the way mothers prepared children for the experience of the infant school.
2 A study of maternal communication to and control over young children.
3 A study of the speech of children aged five through to seven years, with reference to the social factors affecting such speech.
4 The development of an exploratory language programme for working class infant school children.
5 An evaluation of the effects, if any, of such a limited language programme.

At the onset of the research there was no plan for the extension of the study to a middle class population. However, in the August of 1965, a large grant from the Ford Foundation enabled the research to be extended to a sample of middle class parents and to their children, who were going to school for the first time. As a result of this grant a whole new vista of

*University College, London.

1

possibilities opened up quite dramatically. It is, however, important to point out that the first maternal questionnaire, the eliciting contexts for the children's speech, and the questionnaire developed for the teachers were all constructed *before* the middle class sample was obtained.

The research programme was indeed considerable in its breadth and challenging in terms of its problems. It required a rather large research group, spanning the disciplines of sociology, psychology and linguistics. It could not have been carried through without the utter dedication of a young group of researchers who were faced with complex problems both of theory and application at the very beginning of their research career.

The sample: Selection of Schools in the Working Class Area

The area from which the working class sample was obtained is a borough of East London. Its social composition (at least the section in which the sample was drawn) is almost entirely manual working class. The area was chosen because, prior to the research, the Local Education Authority was much concerned with the role of language in education. One major study had already been carried out by the now Senior Educational Psychologist. The Director, the Deputy Director, the Inspector of Primary Schools, and the Educational Psychologist, were all agreed that a large-scale study would be of considerable value. Indeed, the planning of the research involved endless discussion with these officials who gave unstinted time so that a feasible plan could be developed. I doubt whether any research group has enjoyed the co-operation, encouragement and constructive advice which we were so fortunate to receive from the senior officials of the Local Education Authority, in particular from the Deputy Director and the Senior Educational Psychologist. This statement applies even more to the head teachers and teachers of the primary schools.

Our first task was the construction of an experimental design which would allow us to evaluate any consequences of the exploratory language programme. It is a matter of some interest that although only a tiny fraction of the Unit's budget was allocated to this work, the need to evaluate the consequences controlled the major sampling procedures. In terms of the Unit's resources, we could only carry out a language programme in three schools, but the final design called for nine schools. The selection of these nine schools also controlled almost 70% of the families whom we interviewed. It is necessary, therefore, to lay out in some detail the procedures which governed the selection of schools as the latter governed also the character of the sample of mothers and children.

The Selection of Schools (General)

We decided to have two blocks of schools. One block of nine schools was to form the pattern of the experimental design and a block of four schools which we hoped would give us some sociological contrasts to compare with the homogeneity of the schools in the experimental design.

The Sociological Contrast Schools

It is important to remember that when we started we had no idea that we would have the opportunity of a middle class contrast group and we were a little uneasy about the relative social homogeneity of the borough. Consequently four schools were chosen which we hoped would maximise differences in the social class composition of the total sample. We were concerned to include in the sample a lower working class group and a small sub-group who might represent the upper reaches of the working class. With this in mind, we chose four schools. Three of these four schools were located in that part of the borough where it was expected (and it later proved to be the case) that the parents would be placed in a lower socio-economic category than the rest of the sample. The fourth school was selected because the mean I.Q. distribution of the children aged 10+ over a three year period (1960–1962) was somewhat unusual for this borough, in that only 12% of the children had I.Q. scores between 81 – 92 and 42% of the children had I.Q. scores between 108–119. Further, the senior officials of the Local Education Authority told us that the parents of these children were possibly of a relatively higher socio-economic group as many of the parents were home-owning or buying.

Selection of Schools (Specific)

The schools were selected according to the following four criteria:
1 All denominational schools were excluded.
2 All schools with nursery feeders were excluded.
3 The infant and junior departments of the schools were to have separate headmasters or mistresses.
4 The I.Q. distributions of the children in the schools at 10+ were to be similar (this applied only to the nine schools in the experimental design).

Reasons for the Criteria

There was neither time nor researchers to carry out an intensive study of the schools. They had to be selected within the first three months of the research so that we were forced to operate with a priori criteria which we thought would be relevant to the research. Denominational schools were excluded because it was thought that their special characteristics would make comparisons with non-denominational schools invalid. Schools with nursery school feeders were also excluded as the nursery feeders might influence both the children's language and their adjustment to the infant school. It was thought that the overall planning within the school, and the structure of staff relationships within and between the infant and junior departments, would be influenced according to whether there was one head or two. As there were few schools with one head, we decided to accept only those schools where there were two heads. We needed to have some measure of the children within the nine schools which were to make up the experimental design, so we decided to examine the mean I.Q. distribution of the children at 10+ years in the schools for the past three years and choose schools where the mean I.Q. distribution was similar.

The Experimental Design

When all the four criteria were applied to schools who could form part of the experimental design, out of the 37 primary schools in the borough we were left with twelve schools. Of these twelve schools, one was immediately eliminated as it was both a newly built school and it was also regarded in the borough as unusual in its educational approach. When the first group of nine schools for the design was set up we had to exclude one as the internal organization of the school was such that it could not be included in the study. This school, which was originally included in the specific nine schools of the experimental design was streamed, and therefore it was likely that the children would be dispersed at some point of the study. All the schools in the study had to agree to allowing the sample children to remain in the same class for three years. Thus, of the twelve possible schools, we had in the end a total of ten from which we had to choose nine schools.

These nine schools were to be arranged as follows:

The Experimental Schools

In three of the schools we intended to co-operate with the teachers in order to see if we could work out together a limited exploratory language programme, which would encourage the children to become more sensitive to the various uses of language. The teachers of the sample children in these three schools were to meet initially once a week, then once a fortnight, in premises made available by the Local Education Authority, for a period of 1½ to 2 hours, to discuss and work out a language programme. The Local Education Authority very kindly paid these teachers for this extra burden on their time.

4

Control I

A further three of the nine schools were to form the first control group. As with the experimental schools, the teachers of the sample children in each year, formed a small group which met initially once a week and then once a fortnight, in the same premises as the experimental school teachers, but on a different day. This group of teachers was also paid by the Local Education Authority for attendance at these meetings. At these meetings the teachers were to be encouraged to discuss various problems of the education of infant children in their schools. They were also encouraged to investigate these problems provided they could be translated into a *limited* research exercise. In other words an attempt was to be made to heighten the interests of the teachers in the children but no language programme was to be developed. No attempt was ever made in the research to prevent teachers discussing or working towards considerations of language. In fact, such considerations were very rarely brought up by the teachers Control I represented an attempt to build into the design the Hawthorne effect. *I should like to emphasise here most strongly that the experience of both children and of teaching which this group of teachers freely offered made an invaluable contribution to the research.* When these teachers come to read this Monograph, as they will, I would be much saddened if they thought they had played only a subordinate or passive role in the research. This is far from the case. Their knowledge and sensitivity not only prevented us from making more mistakes, it opened up for us many important areas of investigation.

Control II

The final three schools were to be left entirely alone, no exploratory work was to be carried out and no meetings after school were to be arranged with the teachers.

The above experimental design would enable us to evaluate the exploratory language programme because of the range of comparisons between the three groups of schools.

The Allocation of Schools within the Experimental Design

In consultation with the senior officials of the Local Education Authority the ten remaining schools were reduced to nine. By good fortune these nine schools were drawn from three fairly distinct geographical areas within the borough. The three schools in each geographical area were allocated to the experimental group, control group I and control group II by random procedures and then the results were shown to the senior officials of the Local Education Authority for comment. A rather more detailed discussion of the experimental design will be given in a forthcoming monograph by Denis M. and Georgina A. Gahagan who were responsible for the development of the language programme.

After the thirteen schools were chosen, a meeting was arranged to which all the heads of the 37 primary schools were invited. The whole plan of the research was then made fully explicit including the nature of the experimental design. It was explained that no research in schools or interviews of the parents would go forward until the heads had seen and commented upon the procedures to be used or questions to be asked. The meeting was lively and most helpful. The heads gave their permission for the research to begin. I then visited, with one of the officials from the Local Education Authority, each of the selected thirteen schools explaining the school's part in the research. Each head was asked to treat as confidential, the experimental design, which they heard about at the general meeting or at the meeting at the school. I have no reason for believing that this confidence was broken. I should like to take the opportunity (and further opportunities will undoubtedly arise in future monographs) of saying how truly grateful my colleagues and myself are for the patience, steady co-operation, good humour, and timely advice that every headmaster and headmistress offered us throughout the whole life of the research, and we did impose many extra burdens upon each school.

Summary: Selection of Schools

On the basis of four criteria, *nine* schools were selected out of the total of 37 primary schools to form the experimental design. These nine schools were allocated to three groups, an experimental group and two control groups. There was no selection of the teachers of the children.

Four other schools were included in the sample in order to increase the social heterogeneity of the families and children in the total sample. These four schools met three of the sampling criteria for schools. The I.Q. distribution of their children at 10+ was ignored.

The Maternal Interview

After the thirteen schools had been chosen and the heads had agreed through individual meetings to allow us to study their children and the children's parents, the next step was to arrange for the interviewing of the mothers of the children who were going to these schools for the first time in September 1964. However, before discussing the interview with the mothers, we can ask how representative is the sample of families and children in terms of parents and children in the borough as a whole. It is

6

not possible to give an answer to this question because of the various criteria used to select the schools. Although in the sample we had 13 out of the 37 primary schools it should be remembered that all denominational schools were excluded from the sample. This would most certainly have removed from the sample the parents who actively desired their children to go denominational schools. Three out of our thirteen schools were selected to widen the social class differences within the sample. We have no idea whether this proportion approximates to the proportion of lower working class families in the borough. Further, we have only one school which represents a possibly relatively superior sub-group. It is likely that there is an under-representation of families within the sample in the relatively superior socio-economic category of the working class and of white collar parents, in terms of their distribution in the borough as a whole.

I should point out that the probable lack of representation of the selected sample was the direct result of the need to set up an experimental design to evaluate the exploratory language programme. There is a moral here. If research is to serve two very different purposes then the methodology is likely to suffer.

After we had selected the thirteen schools and obtained permission from the heads to carry out the research, we obtained the names of those parents whose children were entering the school to begin their infant school life in September 1964. We interviewed the mothers between the May and August. However, when the children arrived at school we found that a number of the expected children did not in fact arrive, and a number of children were there whom we had not expected. (I should point out there was no selection of children; we took every child who was in that five-year-old intake class and who was at school for the first time.) A second wave of interviewing started immediately, in order to draw into the sample all the parents of the children in that class. As we were very concerned about wastage from the sample across the three years of the research, (we estimated for a 30% wastage rate), in the January when the second school intake took place we added to the sample of parents and their children who arrived in the September class. Thus a small number of interviews took place in the January of 1965.

The Testing of the Children: Ability Tests and Speech Collection

Ability Tests

The Unit sought advice from the N.F.E.R. and Dr. Mittler of Birkbeck College about the tests that were available which were suitable for five-year-old children. Clearly the Unit takes responsibility for the ability tests subsequently used. The Stanford-Binet was ruled out for two reasons. Firstly, we could not afford the cost of administering it and secondly it is not possible to extract from the Binet a measure of so-called non-verbal ability. We decided that what was required was a test of active vocabulary, a test of passive vocabulary and a test of non-verbal ability. The three tests we finally chose after much heart-searching were:

1 The Raven's Progressive Matrices (Children's version) [Non-verbal ability].
2 The English Version of the Peabody Picture Vocabulary Test. [Passive vocabulary].
3 The Crichton Vocabulary Scale. [Active vocabulary].

These three tests were given individually to the children by trained psychologists under the supervision of the Senior Unit Psychologist, Mr. D. Gahagan, to all the children in the thirteen schools after the children had been in school for three weeks. We could not afford to delay the initial testing longer than this as we were concerned with the possible effect of the various schools upon the children's scores. A sub-sample of children was given the three tests after a period of weeks in order to obtain a limited measure of their reliabilities. The Form Board Version of the Raven's Progressive Matrices for Children was then given to a sub-sample of the children in order to compare differences between the children's scores on these two forms of the same test.

The Language Sample

Whilst the ability testing was in progress the first language sample was also obtained from all the children in the thirteen schools. (The details of this sample can be found in the chapters written by Dorothy Henderson in this Monograph.)

So far we have discussed the Unit's work up to Christmas 1964. From January to May, 1965 we were concerned with obtaining samples of the unobserved spontaneous speech of the children to compare with the speech obtained from the language schedule in the October. Telemetering equipment was obtained which made this possible. This equipment consists of a small transmitter about the size of a cigarette box together with a tiny button microphone which the child wears and a receiving unit which can be placed, in principle, up to 100 yards away. The children are free to run about as they wish. We had forty transmitter units and button microphones made but only five of these sets actually worked. It was impossible to distinguish the dummies from the real ones. Forty children drawn from the schools, matched for certain criteria, wore the live transmitters. All the children in each class wore a transmitter but only the transmitter worn by the selected child or children was actually live. The children wore the equipment for two days before the speech was actually recorded. In this way we controlled for the effect of the equipment upon the children. The recordings we have, which vary in amount and quality of speech, give us some picture of a day's speech in the infant school class. The major deficiency of this study is that we could

8

not spare the staff to take down what the child was actually doing throughout the day.

Between May and September, 1965 a number of developments occurred. All the children towards the end of the summer term were given the Wechsler Intelligence Scale for Children (W.I.S.C.) full-scale version. It was administered by psychologists who had received training in the use of this test. The teachers were also asked to fill out a questionnaire concerned to obtain some idea of each child's powers of communication, his general behaviour and the teacher's evaluation of the child's future school career.

The Ford Grant and the Extension of Research in the Middle Class Area

In the middle of this period, July, 1965, the Ford Foundation decided to support the Sociological Research Unit so that a middle class contrast group could be obtained. This was marvellous and opened up magnificent opportunities. The Unit is immensely grateful to the Ford Foundation for adding this dimension to the original research. Between the July and September of 1965, plans were made, a middle class area was selected, the Local Education Authority consulted for permission to carry out the research, schools were selected, head teachers consulted for their co-operation and the mothers were obtained and interviewed. The fact that all this was accomplished within such a short period of time was only possible because of the magnificent co-operation of the Local Education Authority and in particular the Deputy Director, together with the speed of the responsiveness of the head teachers. All this would have been inadequate without the answer to the challenge by the sociologists within the Unit.

The middle class area is drawn from an outlying South East Borough. The borough splits neatly in two, one section of it is broadly working class whilst the other section spans the nuances of the middle class. With the aid of a senior Local Education Authority official who could draw upon a rich knowledge of the borough, five schools were chosen which drew upon different socio-economic categories in their catchment areas. One school was chosen, however, because the majority of the pupils came from an established Local Authority Housing Estate. It was thought at the time that it would be important to compare these working class children and their mothers with working class children and their mothers in the other area. Although this sample does span the levels of the middle class, a deliberate attempt was made to secure an over-representation of the higher levels of the middle class. This was done in order to maximise possible class differences between the two areas. Thus the two samples are in no way representative of the class structure of the society as a whole. We were not concerned with the typicality of the sample population only with the examination of critical differences within it. It is therefore not possible to generalise from our sample to the population as a whole.

9

From September to Christmas 1965, no new data was collected from the working class area, although, of course, the work in the experimental schools continued. In the middle class area we duplicated the first term's work in the working class area. All the children were given the three ability tests and the language of the children was collected. From January to May 1966, apart from some evaluation experiments, no new work was undertaken in the working class area. In the middle class area the spontaneous speech of a specially selected sub-sample of children was collected. Unfortunately, we had difficulty with the equipment and this sample of speech is somewhat inadequate.

Between May and September 1966 there was a spurt of activity. All the children in the middle class area were given the short form of the W.I.S.C. This form was used as we found that the correlation between the short and long form in the working class area was 0.9. Again, in the middle class area the teachers were asked to fill out the identical questionnaire that the teachers in the working class area had filled out one year previously. They were also asked to fill out a second questionnaire which was concerned to obtain information about the kind of discipline the teacher used with each child, and how successful it was. In the working class area in the same period, a second full-scale W.I.S.C. was given to a selected sub-sample of children. The second group of teachers (the children were now in their second year of the infant school) very kindly filled out the questionnaire concerned with the children's powers of communication, their general behaviour, etc., *and* the questionnaire which dealt with the type of discipline the teacher used with each child. Finally, the second speech sample was collected from a selected sub-sample of children in the working class area, who were now at the end of the infant school level.

The Second Speech Sample

There were two major modifications of, and one addition to, the original language schedule used when the children were five years of age.

(a) The Addition
The six questions and three probes which were put to the mothers in order to encourage them to talk freely about how they controlled or disciplined their children were put, with slight modification, to the children. It is therefore possible to compare the mothers' procedures of control with those of the children.

(b) Modifications
1 In the first speech sample, an attempt was made to encourage the children to explain a simple children's game. Difficulties arose in the analysis because the children were allowed to choose one of three possible

10

games and the probes used were inadequate. In the second speech sample, due to the inspiration of Bernard Mohan, linguist in the Sociological Research Unit, a much more reliable and sophisticated context was developed. It was successful both in ensuring that the children understood what was expected of them and in the amount of speech which was produced. The children first of all demonstrated with little figures how the game 'Hide and Seek' is played and gave a running commentary as they did it. Then the researcher took over the figures and the child instructed the researcher in the rules of the game. Finally, all the figures were put away and the child was simply asked how the game was played.

2 In the first speech schedule the child was encouraged to tell a story. The researcher said, "Once upon a time there was a little boy (or girl, depending upon the sex of the child) and all day long he could do anything he wanted. What do you think he did?' There was considerable variability in the children's responses and the method cannot be considered a success. In the second speech schedule a little bear was placed on its side and a sailor, a little boy, a little girl and a dog were put near the bear. The child was told that the bear was going to sleep and the child was invited to tell the bear a story about the sailor, the boy, the girl and a dog. This approach was very successful.

I shall now return to the history of the research.

Within the period September to Christmas 1966 the Neale Reading Test was given to all the working class area children in the sample in the nine schools which made up the pattern of the experimental design. We were also interested in the ability of the children to answer questions of different grammatical form and with varying referents. Dr. Peter Robinson and Susan Rackstraw constructed what they called an 'answering behaviour test' which was given to a selected sub-sample of children. At the same time, a range of experiments was carried out in order to assess the significance of the exploratory language programme.

From January to May 1967 no data was collected from the middle class area. However, further studies were carried out in order to evaluate the language programme in the experimental schools. During this period, the planning, writing and piloting of the second maternal interview took place.

The Second Maternal Interview

This questionnaire was much more ambitious than the first. The first questionnaire, it will be remembered, consisted of pre-determined questions, to which the mother could respond quite freely, concerned with the aspects of the preparation of the child for school — how she controlled the child and answered simple questions the child might put, etc. Her answers were tape-recorded. There were also a number of questions which could be ranked or scaled in the areas of communication, toys, etc. In the

11

second interview we were concerned to establish relationships between:

(a) The decision-making process within the family.
(b) The effect of marriage and children, as constraints upon the development of the mother as a person.
(c) The degree of isolation of the parents from their parents.
(d) The degree of isolation of the family from its community.
(e) The methods of control over the child that were used in a range of different contexts.
(f) The mother's orientation towards the uses of language and communication.
(g) The mother's relationship to the school and aspirations for her child.

We would have liked to have interviewed the fathers but the costs of this would have made such interviewing prohibitive.

From May to September 1967 a series of further evaluation studies of the exploratory language programme were carried out in the experimental design schools. These culminated in a group English General Attainment Test being given to all schools which would permit the use of this test. (Two schools were very hard pressed for time and were unable to co-operate.) In July the second maternal questionnaire was given to all mothers left in the sample in the working class area. *Research in the working class area was now completed.*

In the middle class area, in July, the second language sample was obtained from the children. Between September and Christmas 1967 the second maternal questionnaire was given to all mothers left in the middle class area. The answering behaviour study was also repeated with a sub-group of children matched with those who were chosen for the study in the working class area.

Summary of
The History of the Research
January to May, 1964

Constant discussion with Senior Staff of the L.E.A. throughout this whole period.

1 Meetings with the Head Teachers of all primary schools in the working class area and explanation given of the future research.
2 The creation of the experimental design for the evaluation of the exploratory language programme.
3 The development and piloting of the first maternal interview schedule.

June to September 1964

1 The survey of the mothers.
2 The design of the language programme and its piloting.
3 The start of the meetings with the teachers in the experimental and control I schools. These carried on for the next three years, but were more intermittent in the last year when the children were in the junior school.

September to Christmas 1964

1 Further interviewing of mothers whose children joined the schools in the sample.
2 Three ability tests given to all the sample children. Reliability check on the tests made on a sub-sample of children.
3 The language sample collected from all the children in the thirteen schools.

January to May 1965

1 Small number of mothers interviewed and speech collected from children who joined the schools in the January intake.
2 The spontaneous classroom speech obtained from 40 selected children.

13

1 The full-scale version of the W.I.S.C. given to all the children in the sample.
2 Record of the teaching styles of all the teachers of the sample children obtained.
3 The two teacher questionnaires were constructed and filled in by all teachers at the end of the children's first year in school.
4 Arrival of the Ford Grant.
5 The selection of the middle class area: consultations with senior officials of the L.E.A.: discussion with the head teachers of the five selected schools.
6 Interviewing of the mothers in the middle class area.

September to Christmas 1965
Working class Areas

No data collected.

Middle class Area

1 Three ability tests given to all sample children and the language sample collected after the children had been to school for three weeks.
2 Small number of mothers interviewed whose children had joined the five sample schools.

January to May 1966
Working class Area

No data collected.

Middle class Area

The spontaneous classroom speech of a selected sub-sample of children obtained. Failures in the equipment seriously affected a number of the tapes.

May to September 1966
Working class Area

1 Second full-scale W.I.S.C. given to a selected sub-sample of the children.
2 The two teacher questionnaires given to the second group of teachers of the sample children.

3 Second speech sample collected from a selected sub-sample of the main sample children.

Middle class Area

1 The two teacher questionnaires given to teachers of children who were now completing their first year in the infant school.
2 W.I.S.C. (Short Form) given to all sample children.

September to Christmas 1966
Working class Area

1 The Neale Reading Test given to all children in the nine schools which comprised the experimental design.
2 The answering behaviour study carried out with a selected sub-sample of children.
3 A range of experiments designed to evaluate aspects of the exploratory language programme in the infant school carried out.

Middle class Area

No data collected.

January to May 1967
Working class Area

1 Further evaluation experiments carried out.
2 Planning, writing and piloting of the second maternal questionnaire.

Middle class Area

No data collected.

May to September 1967
Working class Area

1 Final evaluation studies of the exploratory language programme carried out.
2 Group English Attainment Test given to children in all schools who

would co-operate. (Two schools were under great pressure and could not spare the time.)

3 Second interview questionnaire given to all remaining mothers in the original sample.

End of the study of the working class sample.

Middle class Area

1 The second speech sample collected from all the children.
2 The two teacher questionnaires given to the second group of teachers at the end of the children's second year in the infant school.

September to Christmas 1967
Middle class Area

1 Second maternal questionnaire given to all mothers. This interview should have taken place in the summer of 1967 in order to compare strictly with the working class sample. However, as the Ford Grant was due to end in the July, this would have left no time for the analysis. Thus the children of these mothers were about nine months younger than the children of the working class mothers at the time of the second interviews. It was thought that the questions asked in the second interview would not be seriously affected by the discrepancy in the age of the children with the exception of some of the questions which related to the school.

2 The answering behaviour study was repeated with a matched sample of middle class children.

END OF RESEARCH

Chapter I

SOCIAL CLASS DIFFERENCES IN FORM-CLASS USAGE AMONG FIVE-YEAR-OLD CHILDREN
D. Henderson

Introduction

In the preface to this monograph Basil Bernstein gave an outline of the first speech sample obtained from the five-year-old children in the survey. In this and the following chapter we shall give an analysis of the factors which affected the 'vocabulary' the children used when they were given the opportunity to talk about several different tasks. We have chosen to use the term 'form-class' in preference to 'vocabulary' or 'lexicon' because strictly speaking some of the words we examined could be considered items of grammar.*

A number of different analyses have been carried out on the speech we collected from 150 children in the middle class area and 300 children in the working class area.

(1) The form-class usage across three tasks of a specially selected sub-sample of children.

(2) Differences in the allocation of these form classes between three tasks.

(3) A detailed grammatical analysis of the speech of the sub-sample children across the tasks and between the tasks.

(4) A grammatical analysis of the *total* sample of children was developed in order to point up social class differences in the children's grammar.

In this monograph we shall be concerned with (1) and (2). As we had a fairly large sample of children we had an opportunity to compare the possible influences of a range of factors upon the children's speech.

A We could examine the effect of the sex of the children upon their speech.

B We could examine the effect of the social class position of the children's parents upon the children's speech.

C We could compare the effect of differences in the measured ability of the children upon their speech.

D We could find out whether the score on an index of the mother's reported communications to her child, obtained during the maternal

*See Appendix: 'Criteria for Classifying the Form Classes'.

survey in the previous summer had any relation to the speech the children produced.

We were also very concerned to examine the effects of the interactions among social class, sex, ability of the child and the mother's communication index score. In order to be able to make such comparisons a factorial design was drawn up and children were selected from the main sample according to the above criteria to fill the factorial design's various cells.

Previous research carried out in the Unit, and of course other research, suggested that of all the variables listed above, social class would appear as the one which would have the most powerful relation with the form-class usage of the children. We believed that the ability of the child would have a weaker relation to the children's speech than social class. We also thought that when a relationship existed between the child's ability and his speech it would be affected by his parent's social class position. High ability middle class children might produce higher scores on our various measures than, for example, average ability middle class children. We, therefore, did not expect such clear differences within the working class sample between high and average ability children. We considered that the sex of the child would also affect his scores on the various measures. Girls as a group we expected would score higher than boys, but we thought that the differences between boys and girls in the working class would be greater than the differences between boys and girls in the middle class. We were less sure of the effect of the mother's score on the index of *reported* communication to her child as this index was based upon her report, not upon her actual behaviour. Further, this index was based upon only *two* measures of the mother's reported communications to her child as we did not develop the final index of maternal communication and control until over one year later. However, we used the simple index in the factorial design since, crude as it is, it represented a possible influencing factor. There will be a detailed discussion of these anticipations in the body of the chapter.

We believe that the study we are presenting here is unique in terms of the matching of the children for social class, sex, three ability levels and a measure of maternal communication *and* in terms of the uniform contexts used to elicit various forms of speech.

The language of the body of the report is somewhat formal. This is because the analysis is complicated and it was felt necessary to spell out very explicitly its various stages. This does involve some repetition but it was thought that if such repetitions were an aid to clarity then they were of value.

The Factorial Sample

The total number of five-year-old children in the first speech sample was 450. Of these children 300 came from the working class area and 150 came from the middle class area. The very size of this sample allowed us to select a sub-sample of children who could be closely matched on a range of variables which we considered might influence their speech. Because we wanted to be able to examine the various interactions between groups of children matched for social class, sex, verbal ability and their mothers' communication index score, we drew up a factorial design which originally called for sixty middle class children and sixty working class children. Within each social class the children were divided into equal numbers of boys and girls and each group of boys and girls was divided into three verbal ability groups: high, medium and low verbal ability. Finally, because we were interested to see whether the mothers' communication index scores affected the children's speech within each social class, sex and ability level, the children were divided into two groups according to whether their mothers were high or low on the Communication Index. Thus the factorial design created 24 cells each containing five children who shared the same sex, ability level and social class and whose mothers had similar Communication Index scores. When we applied these criteria to the whole sample of children we found that there were *no* low ability middle class children whose mothers received *low* Communication Index scores. Thus the final factorial design contained only 22 cells instead of the desired 24 cells and the middle class sample of the children was reduced by ten to 50 children.

We shall first discuss the criteria we used to allocate children according to social class, verbal ability scores and Communication Index scores. Secondly, we shall describe the criteria and procedures for obtaining the children's speech (the speech schedule). Thirdly, we shall describe the three tasks which form the basis of the analysis of the speech and discuss the definition of the form classes. We will then be in a position to consider the statistical analysis that we used and to give a report of the findings.

The criteria used to allocate children to social class, verbal ability and communication index groups

A Social Class

The criteria used to determine the social class ratings of the children were the terminal education and occupation of both parents. A full description of the criteria used in the construction of the scale is given in the Appendix dealing with the Index of Social Class by W. Brandis.

Within the factorial samples the social class distribution was as follows:

19

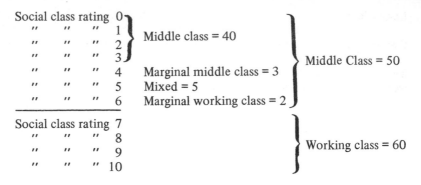

Social class rating 0 ⎫
       "   "   " 1 ⎬ Middle class = 40
       "   "   " 2 ⎭
       "   "   " 3   Middle Class = 50
       "   "   " 4   Marginal middle class = 3
       "   "   " 5   Mixed = 5
       "   "   " 6   Marginal working class = 2

Social class rating 7
       "   "   " 8
       "   "   " 9   Working class = 60
       "   "   " 10

Factorial sample = 110

B The Communication Index

This Index was based upon the combined scores from two closed schedules concerned with aspects of communication between mother and child. The first schedule assessed the willingness of the mother to take up her child's attempts at verbal interaction across a range of behavioural settings. The second schedule assessed the extent to which the mother would avoid or evade answering difficult questions put to her by the child. A factor analysis was carried out which justified the scoring procedures used. Thus a high score on this Index represented a mother who indicated that she would verbally respond to her child's attempts to chat to her in a range of contexts, and who would explain rather than avoid answering difficult questions put to her by her child. A ten-point scale 0–9 was produced.*

C Verbal Ability Scores

All the children in the main sample were given two verbal ability tests after they had been in school for three weeks. The tests chosen were the Crichton Vocabulary Scale and the English Version of the Peabody Picture Vocabulary Test. The Crichton Vocabulary Scale was considered to be the most appropriate test because it was a test of active vocabulary. The tests were administered individually to each child by a qualified psychologist. Children who were placed in the category defined as High verbal ability had scores at the 90th percentile or better on the Crichton Vocabulary Scale. Children who were placed in the category defined as Medium verbal ability had scores between the 50th percentile and the 75th percentile. Children placed in the category defined as Low verbal ability had scores at the 25th percentile or below on the Crichton Vocabulary Scale.

---

*A description of the schedules and the scoring used in the construction of the Communication Index is given in the Appendix by W. Brandis.

Limitations

Owing to some difficulties in matching on the Crichton Vocabulary Scale, the score on the English Version of the Peabody Picture Vocabulary Test had to be used as the matching criterion for 11 children, eight of whom were middle class children and three working class children.

The sample was sub-divided into High Communication Index children and Low Communication Index children, according to their mothers' ratings on the Communication Index scale. The groups were further sub-divided three ways in terms of verbal ability test scores. This was not possible in the case of the middle class Low Communication Index groups. These middle class Low Communication Index groups were sub-divided two ways into a High and a Medium ability group. We made an effort to maximise the social class contrasts in the sample. However, the 10 children with social class ratings of 4, 5 and 6 had to be included in the middle class group. This means that the middle class group in the factorial sample is not as homogeneous a class group as the working class group.

The limitations of the matching are presented in Table 1.

TABLE 1

Mean Scores for the Matching Criteria used in the Factorial Sample

	Middle Class = 2.3 (N = 50)			Mean Social
	Working Class = 7.5 (N = 60)			Class Rating

	High	Medium	Low	
Middle Class:	90.3	63.5	18.0⎱	Mean Verbal
Working Class:	90.0	53.0	10.3⎰	Ability Score

	High	Low	
Middle Class:	6.9	4.9⎱	Mean Maternal Com
Working Class:	6.3	3.6⎰	munication Index Score

It can be seen that the matching of ability scores for Medium and Low groups is such that the middle class children have higher mean scores in these two ranges than the working class children. It will be shown later that this discrepancy does not invalidate the results. It is also the case that the working class Low Maternal Communication Index score is lower than the Low Maternal Communication Index score of the middle class group.

Despite these limitations the design does allow for a reasonable control on all the variables which were expected to influence the speech of the children available at the time of the analysis. To our knowledge no other language study in this country has utilised such controls in the examination of the speech of children.

21

TABLE 2

The Factorial Design

(N = 110)

	MIDDLE CLASS			WORKING CLASS		
	High V.A. Boys Girls	Medium V.A. Boys Girls	Low V.A. Boys Girls	High V.A. Boys Girls	Medium V.A Boys Girls	Low V.A. Boys Girls
High Communi-cation Index	N N 5 5	N N 5 5	N N 5 5	N N 5 5	N N 5 5	N N 5 5
Low Communi-cation	N N 5 5	N N 5 5		N N 5 5	N N 5 5	N N 5 5

The Speech Schedule: Description of the Tasks

All the children in the main sample were given the speech schedule during their third week in school. The speech schedule, which was initally piloted on 40 children of similar age to the sample children, was made up of six different tasks. These tasks were specifically chosen to obtain a varied selection of types of speech from five-year-old children. All the tasks were considered to be of interest to young children. Care was taken to control the level of difficulty of these tasks so that all the children would be able to talk freely.

1 The Model Room
The equipment for this task was a set of doll's living-room furniture, together with four small dolls (a man, a woman, a boy and a girl).

2 The Picture Story Cards
This task consisted of three sets of picture story cards. Each set contained four cards or frames. The first set of cards showed some children playing football and breaking a window. The second set of cards showed a boy fishing and falling into the water. The third set of cards showed a cat stealing some fish.

3 The Trotin Cards
This task consisted of three postcards which were reproductions of the work of a Belgian painter Trotin. Each card depicted a different scene. All the cards were highly detailed and very colourful. The first Trotin card showed a train start:ng in a crowded station. The second Trotin card showed a more static scene; a number of people seated around a large and well-laden table in a garden. This card showed other people variously occupied in the garden and outside a house. The third Trotin card showed a street scene. This card depicted a variety of activities in the street and outside shops and stalls.

22

4 Imaginative Story Completion

Here, the interviewer simply said, 'This is a story about a little boy (or girl, depending upon the sex of the child being interviewed) who could do what he (or she) liked for a whole day. What do you think he (or she) did?' The child was then invited to tell a story.

5 Explanation of Games

The interviewer asked the child if he or she had ever played 'Hide and Seek' and 'Musical Chairs'. If the child said that he or she had played these games, the interviewer asked the child to tell her how to play them. If neither of these games was familiar to the child, he or she was asked to explain a game with which he or she *was* familiar.

6 The Elephant

This was a small mechanical elephant. The elephant carried a drum and cymbals. The cymbals were attached to the end of the elephant's trunk and the top of the drum, and the drum was fixed to the front of the elephant. The drumsticks were attached to the end of the elephant's arms. When a rubber bulb at the end of a tube, which was connected to the toy was depressed, the elephant banged the drum and the cymbals simultaneously.

Presentation of the Tasks

The interviews with the children took place in their schools during the third week after the beginning of their first term. Each researcher spent one day in the child's classroom before collecting speech from the child. The researchers were asked to be warm, friendly and receptive during the interviews with the children. They were told not to ask additional questions which would increase the complexity of the situation, but were told to offer positive reinforcement between the tasks and to tolerate silences. In the case of the working class children, the interviewers offered additional reinforcement to create better rapport and because of this there was some departure from the schedule. A number of uncontrolled comments were also made by the interviewers. However, this analysis of the speech is strictly limited to the children's responses to the *formal* questions and *probes*. Despite the departures from the schedule, the speech is controlled in the analysis. In the case of the middle class children, no such departures from the schedule occurred. Thus the situation for the working class children was less formal and more verbal interaction occurred between interviewer and child. There was no overall difference between the amount of task-relevant speech offered by middle class and working class children. All five interviewers were women, three of whom were researchers in the Unit, and two had experience as infant school teachers.

23

Since the children were so young, and new to the school situation, a positive effort was made to mitigate fatigue. The children were interviewed only between the period immediately following milk-time, and before playtime in the afternoon. We thought that interviewing after break in the afternoon would unduly fatigue the children. The children were not prevented from talking in any way, even when their speech was irrelevant to the task in hand. When this happened, the researcher gently redirected the child's attention to the task. Each child was interviewed separately in a small room provided by the school. The schedule took approximately 30 minutes to present but no time limit was set.*

1 The Model Room

The child was given the furniture and room-base and asked to arrange a room — 'Just like the room in *your* house'. The interviewer then handed the child the four dolls and asked the child to put them in the room where he or she liked. The child was then asked to tell the interviewer what they were doing, what they were talking about and what they were saying to each other. This sequence was repeated with the dolls seated around the table, and with the adult dolls in the armchairs.†

2 The Picture Story Cards

Each set of picture story cards was shown to the child one at a time, in the following order:

(i)   Football
(ii) Fishing
(iii) Cat and Fish

The cards (or frames) in each set were laid down on the table, in front of the child, fairly slowly, so that they formed a picture strip. The interviewer told the child that the pictures told a story, and a one-sentence summary of the story was given by the interviewer. The child was then invited to tell the story. If the child stopped after any card, the interviewer directed his or her attention to the next card, and asked what happened next. At the end of each story the interviewer pointed to some of the characters in the story and asked the child what each character was saying.

3 The Trotin Cards

The child was given one picture at a time. When the interviewer had placed the picture on the table in front of child, she asked the child to tell what was going on in the picture, then, what was happening in the picture. If

*If the child clearly refused to respond to the first task he or she was taken back to the classroom and ten days later a second attempt was made. All children completed the speech schedule (see data on total refusals).

†One of the aims of this section was simply to provide the children with a task which was enjoyable and which would make very few linguistic demands upon them and thus help to establish rapport between the interviewer and the child.

the child gave little verbal response to these questions, the interviewer asked the child what he or she could see, and also what the people were doing. When the child stopped speaking, the interviewer asked what else was going on. Finally, the child was asked to give a name to the picture. This formula was followed with each of the three cards.

4 Story Completion

The interviewer started to tell a story to the child, saying, 'Once upon a time, there was a little boy (or girl), and for a whole day he (or she) could do anything he (or she) wanted to...... what do you think he (or she) did?' The child was then invited to develop the story and complete it.

5 Explanation of Games

The interviewer asked the child if he or she had ever played 'Hide and Seek' and 'Musical Chairs'. If the child said he or she had played either of these games, he or she was asked to tell the interviewer how it was played. The interviewer told the child that she could not play the game. If the child found the explanation difficult to begin, the interviewer asked, 'How does it start?'. If the child found difficulty in continuing the explanation, the interviewer asked: 'How does it go on?' Only one of these two probes was allowed.

If the child said that he or she had not played either of these games, the interviewer asked the child what games he or she played, and which was best liked. The game mentioned by the child was treated in exactly the same way.

6 The Elephant

The interviewer showed the toy to the child and asked the child what it was. The interviewer named specific parts of the toy, then she pointed to each named part, asking: 'What's this?'

The toy was then worked by the interviewer and then given to the child, who was told that they were going to play a game. The interviewer blindfolded herself and asked the child to tell her what the elephant was doing. When the child stopped speaking, the interviewer was instructed to probe further, saying: 'Is there anything else happening?' Finally, the interviewer asked the child how the elephant worked and then, what made it work.

All the interviews with the children were tape-recorded. No speech that occurred during the interviewing was omitted from the tapes. Each interview was transcribed verbatim. Each transcription was then rechecked against the tape-recording and necessary alterations and amendments were made.

25

The Form Classes, their Definitions and the Selected Tasks

We are concerned with the differences between the scores in the sub-classes in the factorial design on nine measures. Each measure was summed over three tasks for each child. The measures are:

(1) The total number of task-relevant words produced by each child when talking about the three tasks.

(2) The total number of words in each of the following form-classes, produced by each child:
    1 The total number of nouns
    2 The total number of verbs*
    3 The total number of adverbs
    4 The total number of adjectives

(3) The total number of different words, in each of the following form-class† produced by each child:
    1 The total number of different nouns
    2 The total number of different verbs
    3 The total number of different adverbs
    4 The total number of different adjectives

The score for different nouns, adjectives, verbs and adverbs was calculated by summing the number of different nouns, etc. used on each task. Each task was considered as a fresh context.‡

The Analysis of Form-Classes

For the purpose of the analysis of form-classes, three of the tasks in the speech schedule were examined. These were:

(1) The Picture Story Cards
(2) The Trotin Cards
(3) The Elephant

*An examination of the form class verbs showed that the verb 'to be' was used very frequently. It was thought that this item might be inflating the token verb count. It was therefore decided to re-analyse the token verb count, omitting the verb 'to be'. However, the differential frequency of the verb 'to be' was also analysed separately.

†The criteria for the classification of the form classes was derived from Fries and Strang. These are described in the Appendix to this section.

‡The residual number of words was also determined for each child, that is, the number of task-relevant words that remained when the totals for token nouns, token verbs, token adjectives and token adverbs were summed and deducted from total task-relevant speech. However, the residual number of words is not necessarily the same as the total number of words the child produced across the three tasks. Variations in the total number of form-class words produced by each child would clearly affect the number of residual words where the total number of words was the same. On the other hand, similar total form-class scores would give different residual speech scores where the total number of words produced across the three tasks varied. It was therefore decided to exclude this confusing category from the analysis.

These three tasks were chosen from the six in the schedule because it was considered that these tasks would be likely to elicit three different types of speech:

  (a) The Picture Story Cards   — narrative speech
  (b) The Trotin Cards   — descriptive speech
  (c) The Elephant   — explanatory speech

The other tasks were much more open and it was thought that the responses of the children would be much less controlled.

The Statistical Analysis

Lists were made of the words in each form-class used by each child on each of the three tasks. The number of times each word was used by each child on each task was then calculated. The total number of different words (types) in each form-class was found by summing the number of different words used in each task. The total number of words (tokens) in each form-class, was found by summing *all* words in each form-class *across* the three tasks. Each child in the factorial sample now had scores for each of the nine measures. The scores for each cell in the factorial sample were summed, and the means for each cell were found for each of the nine measures.

It was decided to conduct analyses of variance on the data. However, because of the absence of cells containing Low Communication Index, Low verbal ability middle class children in the factorial sample, three over-lapping analyses of variance had to be carried out for each measure. Only in this way could all the comparisons be considered. These three separate analyses of variance will be referred to as the sub-samples.

TABLE 3

Sub-sample 1 (N = 80)

	Middle class				Working class			
	High V.A.		Medium V.A.		High V.A.		Medium V.A.	
High Communication Index	Boys	Girls	Boys	Girls	Boys	Girls	Boys	Girls
Low Communication Index	Boys	Girls	Boys	Girls	Boys	Girls	Boys	Girls

Sub-sample 2 (N = 60)

	Middle class						Working class					
	High V.A.		Medium V.A.		Low V.A.		High V.A.		Medium V.A.		Low V.A.	
High Communication Index	Boys	Girls	Boys	Girls	Boys	Girls	Boys	Girls	Boys	Girls	Boys	Girls

27

TABLE 3 (Contd.)

Sub-sample 3 (N = 60)

	Working Class		
	High V.A.	Medium V.A.	Low V.A.
High Communication Index	Boys Girls	Boys Girls	Boys Girls
Low Communication Index	Boys Girls	Boys Girls	Boys Girls

Composition of each sub-sample for the Analysis of Variance

(1) Sub-sample 1 excluded all Low verbal ability children and contained middle and working class High and Medium verbal ability children with High and Low Maternal Communication Index ratings.

(2) Sub-sample 2 excluded all Low Maternal Communication Index children, and contained all the High Communication Index children in the sample.

(3) Sub-sample 3 excluded all middle class children and contained all the working class children in the sample.

(It was impossible to analyse the middle class sample separately because of the omission of Low verbal ability, Low Communication Index middle class children.)

The Sign Test

A sign test based on the median scores for each of the nine measures was also carried out. We thought that such a sign test might give a clear, albeit crude, overall picture of the general tendencies, and it enabled us to consider *all* the cells in the factorial sample as a whole.

Results of the Analyses of Variance

These results will be discussed in terms of:

(a) Main order differences within each of the three sub-samples.

(b) Interactions within each sub-sample.

Each sub-sample will be dealt with separately. The analysis of the total task speech within each cell of each sub-sample revealed no significant differences. We analysed the form-classes on the basis of raw scores.

28

Main order Differences within the Sub-samples.

Sub-sample I

This sample excluded all the Low verbal ability children in the factorial sample, and included middle and working class High and Medium verbal ability children with High and Low Maternal Communication Index ratings. The results will be discussed in terms of each of the form-class measures.

Nouns

The major difference in the use of token nouns and type nouns was related to social class. Middle class children produced significantly more token nouns than working class children ($F_{1,64}$ = 8.8, p < .01). They also produced more different nouns than working class children and this result is at a higher level of significance ($F_{1,64}$ = 19.2, p < .001).

Verbs

Social class, sex and Communication Index were associated with significant differences in the use of token verbs, the use of 'to be', and the use of different verbs. Middle class children produced significantly more token verbs (the verb 'to be' included) than working class children ($F_{1,64}$ = 25.9 p < .001). Sex differences were found in the use of token verbs (verb 'to be' included). Boys used significantly more token verbs than girls ($F_{1,64}$ = 7.2, p < .01). Low Communication Index children used significantly more token verbs (verb 'to be' included) than High Communication Index children ($F_{1,64}$ = 6.2, p < .025).

However, as it was thought that the token verb count could have been swollen by the use of the verb 'to be', a second token verb count was carried out in which the verb 'to be' was excluded. It was then found that there were *no* significant differences in the use of token verbs minus the verb 'to be', associated with social class, sex or the Communication Index comparisons.

The analysis of the differential frequency with which the verb 'to be' was used, showed that middle class children used the verb 'to be' significantly more than working class children ($F_{1,64}$ = 6.2, p < .025). Boys used the verb 'to be' significantly more than girls ($F_{1,64}$ = 5.6, p < .025). Low Communication Index children used the verb 'to be' significantly more than High Communication Index children ($F_{1,64}$ = 5.6, p < .025).

In the case of type verbs, middle class children used significantly more type verbs than working class children ($F_{1,64}$ = 4.7, p < .05).

Adverbs

The differences in the use of token adverbs and type adverbs were related to verbal ability scores.

Medium verbal ability children used significantly more token adverbs

29

than High verbal ability children ($F_{1,64} = 9.1$, p $<$ .01). (It will be remembered that Low verbal ability children were excluded from this sub-sample.) Medium verbal ability children were also found to use significantly more type adverbs than High verbal ability children ($F_{1,64} = 9.7$, p $<$ .01).

Adjectives
No significant differences in the use of token adjectives were found in the analysis of this sub-sample, but middle class children used significantly more type adjectives than working class children ($F_{1,64} = 9.8$, p $<$ .01). The use of type adjectives was also related to the sex of the child. Girls used more different adjectives than boys ($F_{1,64} = 4.1$, p $<$ .05).

Summary
In this sub-sample, the major differences in the use of token nouns, type nouns, token verbs, use of the verb 'to be', type verbs and type adjectives were *not* related to the verbal ability scores of the children but to the *social class* of their parents. Middle class children scored significantly more on all these measures than did working class children. Girls used type adjectives more frequently than boys, but boys used token verbs, and the verb 'to be' more frequently than girls. Low Communication Index scores were related to the use of token verbs, and the use of the verb 'to be'. The only relationship found between verbal ability scores and form-class usage was in the use of token adverbs and type adverbs. Children of Medium verbal ability were found to have higher scores on these measures than children of High verbal ability.

Sub-sample 2
This sample excluded all Low Communication Index children and contained all High Communication Index children.

Nouns
It was found that *middle class* High Communication Index children produced significantly more token nouns than working class High Communication Index children ($F_{1,48} = 6.9$, p $<$ .025). Middle class High Communication Index children also produced significantly more type nouns than working class High Communication Index children ($F_{1,48} = 15.3$, p $<$ .001).

Verbs
No significant differences in the use of token verbs, the use of 'to be' or the use of type verbs, were found in this sub-sample.

Adverbs
No significant differences in the use of token adverbs, or in the use of type adverbs were found in this sub-sample.

30

Adjectives
No significant differences were found, in this sub-sample, in the use of token adjectives, but it was found that middle class High Communication Index children used significantly more type adjectives than working class High Communication Index children ($F_{1,48} = 6.4$, p < .025). The use of type adjectives was also related to the sex of the children. High Communication Index girls used significantly more type adjectives than High Communication Index boys ($F_{1,48} = 6.1$, p < .025).

Summary
It should be noted that in this sub-sample the Communication Index is held constant for all the children. The comparisons are between children who *all* share High Communication Index scores.

No relationship was found, in this sub-sample, between verbal ability scores and the use of the various form-classes. Social class is related to the use of token nouns, type nouns and type adjectives. Middle class children used more than working class children. Girls used more type adjectives than boys. *The effect of controlling for High Communication Index reduced the number of significant differences.* The significant differences found in the use of type verbs, token verbs and token adverbs, in Sub-sample 1, disappeared.

Sub-sample 3
This sample excluded all middle class children, and thus represents *the working class sample.*

Nouns
No significant differences were found, in the working class sub-sample, in the use of token or type nouns.

Verbs
No significant differences were found within this sub-sample in the use of token or type verbs, or in the use of 'to be'.

Adverbs
Differences in the use of token adverbs were found between High and Low Communication Index children and between the verbal ability groups. No differences were found, in this sub-sample, in the use of type adverbs. Working class High Communication Index children were found to use significantly more token adverbs than working class Low Communication Index children ($F_{1,48} = 7.8$, p < .01). Working class Medium verbal ability children produced significantly more token adverbs than High or Low verbal ability working class children ($F_{2,48} = 10.3$, p < .001).

Adjectives
Working class girls used significantly more token adjectives than working class boys ($F_{1,48} = 8.9$, p < .01).

31

They also used significantly more type adjectives than working class boys ($F_{1,48} = 12.4$, p $<$ .01).

Summary
Within this sub-sample of working class children, no significant differences were found in the use of token nouns, type nouns, token verbs, use of the verb 'to be', type verbs or type adverbs. High Communication Index children used token adverbs more frequently than Low Communication Index children, and children of Medium verbal ability used this form-class more frequently than children of High or Low verbal ability. Working class girls used more token adjectives and more type adjectives than did working class boys.

Interactions within the Sub-Samples

Sub-Sample 1

Nouns
The interaction between social class and verbal ability was significant in the case of both token nouns and type nouns. Middle class children with High verbal ability used significantly more token nouns ($F_{1,64} = 4.6$, p $<$ .05), and significantly more type nouns ($F_{1,64} = 4.6$, p $<$ .05).

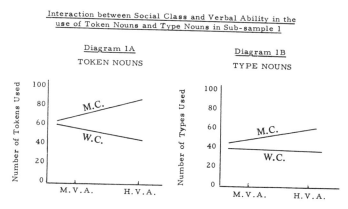

Interaction between Social Class and Verbal Ability in the use of Token Nouns and Type Nouns in Sub-sample 1

Diagram 1A
TOKEN NOUNS

Diagram 1B
TYPE NOUNS

Verbs
Significant interactions between social class and verbal ability were also found in the use of token verbs and in the use of the verb 'to be'. In this sub-sample no significant interaction occurred in the case of type verbs. Middle class High verbal ability children used more token verbs ($F_{1,64} = 37.5$, p $<$ .001), and used the verb 'to be' more frequently ($F_{1,64} = 5.1$, p $<$ .05).

32

Interaction between Social Class and Verbal Ability in the use of Token Verbs and in the use of 'to be' in Sub-Sample 1

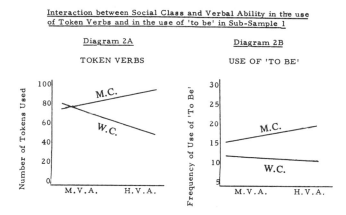

Diagram 2A

TOKEN VERBS

Diagram 2B

USE OF 'TO BE'

The use of token verbs and the use of the verb 'to be' was a function of the interaction between social class and sex. Middle class boys were found to have high scores in their use of token verbs ($F_{1,64} = 11.7$, $p < .01$) and in their use of the verb 'to be' ($F_{1,64} = 4.3$, $p < .05$).

Interaction between Social Class and Sex in the use of Token Verbs and in the use of 'to be' in Sub-Sample 1

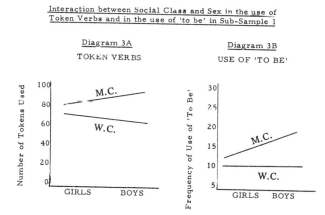

Diagram 3A

TOKEN VERBS

Diagram 3B

USE OF 'TO BE'

The interaction between sex and Communication Index was significant in the case of token verbs and in the use of the verb 'to be'. Low Communication Index boys were found to have high scores in their use of token verbs ($F_{1,64} = 5.7$, $p < .025$), and in their use of the verb 'to be' ($F_{1,64} = 5.1$, $p < .05$).

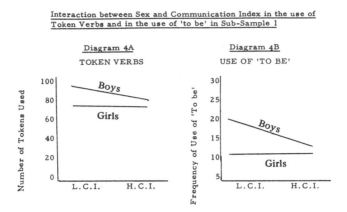

Interaction between Sex and Communication Index in the use of
Token Verbs and in the use of 'to be' in Sub-Sample 1

Diagram 4A

TOKEN VERBS

Diagram 4B

USE OF 'TO BE'

The interaction between verbal ability and Communication Index was significant in the case of token verbs. High verbal ability, Low Communication Index children were found to produce high scores in their use of token verbs ($F_{1,64} = 25.9$, p $<$ .001).

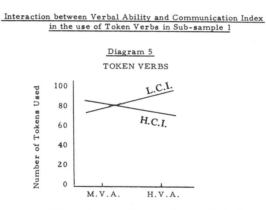

Interaction between Verbal Ability and Communication Index
in the use of Token Verbs in Sub-sample 1

Diagram 5

TOKEN VERBS

However, no significant interactions were revealed when the token verb count, minus the verb 'to be', was re-analysed.

Adverbs
No significant interactions were revealed in the use of token adverbs or in the use of type adverbs in this sub-sample.

Adjectives
The interaction between social class and verbal ability was significant in the case of type adjectives. No significant interactions were found in the case of token adjectives. Middle class High verbal ability children showed high scores in their use of type adjectives ($F_{1,64} = 4.6$, p $<$ .05).

34

Diagram 6

TYPE ADJECTIVES

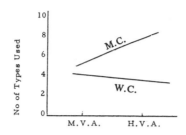

Summary

There were no significant interaction effects when the verb 'to be' was omitted from the token verb count. There were no significant interaction effects in the use of token adverbs and type adverbs, token adjectives and type verbs. Middle class children of High verbal ability used more token nouns and more type nouns and more type adjectives. The major interaction effect was between social class and verbal ability scores.

Sub-sample 2

Nouns
There were no significant interaction effects in the use of token nouns and type nouns.

Verbs
There was no significant interaction effects in the use of token verbs, token verbs minus 'to be', the use of 'to be' or type verbs.

Adverbs
There were no significant interaction effects in the use of token adverbs or type adverbs.

Adjectives
The interaction between social class and verbal ability scores was significant in the case of type adjectives. No significant interactions were found in the use of token adjectives.

Middle class High verbal ability children showed high scores in the use of type adjectives ($F_{2,48} = 5.1$, p $<$ .01).

35

Diagram 7

TYPE ADJECTIVES

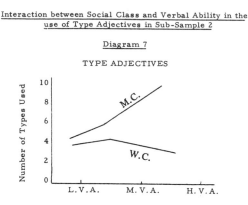

Summary
In this sub-sample, it will be remembered, the comparisons are made between children who *all* share High Communication Index ratings. The only interaction effect was in the use of type adjectives. Here middle class children of High verbal ability used more type adjectives. Thus, when the Communication Index was held constant, middle class children of High verbal ability were found to offer more type adjectives.

Sub-sample 3
Nouns
No significant interactions were found in the use of token nouns or in the use of type nouns.

Verbs
No significant interactions were found in the use of token verbs, the use of the verb 'to be', or the use of different verbs.

Adverbs
A significant interaction effect occurred between verbal ability scores and Communication Index in the use of token adverbs. No significant inter-

Interaction of Verbal Ability and Communication Index in
the use of Token Adverbs in Sub-Sample 3

Diagram 8

TOKEN ADVERBS

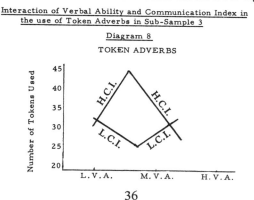

actions were found in the use of type adverbs. High Communication Index, Medium verbal ability children were found to have high token adverb scores ($F_{2,48} = 3.8$, p $<$ .05).

Adjectives

No significant interactions were found in the use of token adjectives or in the use of type adjectives.

Summary

The only interaction effect found in the working class sub-sample is between verbal ability scores and Communication Index ratings. High Communication Index children with Medium verbal ability scores were found to use more token adverbs. This is the only case of a significant interaction effect in the use of token adverbs in the analyses of the three sub-samples.

Note to the Analysis of Variance

The analysis of variance reveals the general overall higher scores of middle class children on most of the form-class measures. Inspection of the data, however, led to the view that working class children as a *whole* appear to be using more token adverbs. We therefore decided to test the significance of the move of working class children to token adverbs. The only way in which this could be carried out in order to include *all* the children in the sample simultaneously was to make a simple comparison between *all* middle class children and *all* working class children. A t-test on the significance of the mean difference between the scores on token adverbs for the middle class and working class children revealed that working class children tended to use more token adverbs than middle class children, and that this tendency was significant (t = 2.18, p $<$ .05).

A final point should be made in the consideration of the results revealed by the analysis of variance. Significant differences which were found in more than one sub-sample are consistent in the direction of the difference. Conflicting results did not appear in the three sub-samples.

The Results of the Sign Test

The median score for each of the nine measures (total task speech, token nouns, type nouns, token verbs*, type verbs, token adverbs, type adverbs, token adjectives and type adjectives) for the *whole* sample was obtained.

*The use of the verb 'to be' was *not* excluded from the token verb measure in the sign test, and therefore it should be remembered that this measure was swollen by 'listing' behaviour on the part of middle-class boys whose mothers had Low Communication Index ratings.

FACTORIAL DESIGN

	MIDDLE CLASS						WORKING CLASS						
	High Verbal Ability		Medium Verbal Ability		Low Verbal Ability		High Verbal Ability		Medium Verbal Ability		Low Verbal Ability	
	Boys	Girls	Boys	Girls	Boys	Girls	Boys	Girls	Boys	Girls	Boys	Girls
High Communication Index	5 S.S.1* S.S.2	5 S.S.1 S.S.2	5 S.S.1 S.S.2	5 S.S.1 S.S.2	5 S.S.2	5 S.S.2	5 S.S.1 S.S.2 S.S.3	5 S.S.1 S.S.2 S.S.3	5 S.S.1 S.S.2 S.S.3	5 S.S.1 S.S.2 S.S.3	5 S.S.2 S.S.3	5 S.S.2 S.S.3
Low Communication Index	5 S.S.1	5 S.S.1	5 S.S.1	5 S.S.1			5 S.S.1 S.S.3	5 S.S.1 S.S.3	5 S.S.1 S.S.3	5 S.S.1 S.S.3	5 S.S.3	5 S.S.3

* The symbols within each cell indicate the inclusion of that cell in a particular sub-sample.

TABLE 4

Median Scores which formed the basis for the Sign Test

Form-Class	Median Score
Token Nouns	71.2
Type Nouns	43.1
Token Verbs	83.4
Type Verbs	38.8
Token Adverbs	32.0
Type Adverbs	16.3
Token Adjectives	7.4
Type Adjectives	4.6
Total Task Speech	405.4

Cells (the groups of five children) with mean scores *below* the median for each measure are denoted by a minus sign and cells with mean scores *above* the median are denoted by a plus sign.

TABLE 5

MIDDLE CLASS

	High Communication Index						Low Communication Index				Total x̄ Score above Median
	High V.A.		Med. V.A.		Low V.A.		High V.A.		Med. V.A.		
	Boys	Girls	Boys	Girls	Boys	Girls	Boys	Girls	Boys	Girls	
Total Task Speech	+	+	+	-	-	-	+	-	-	-	4
Token Nouns	+	+			-	+	+	-	+	-	5
Type Nouns	+	+	-	-	-	-	+	-	+	-	4
Token Verbs	+	-	-	-	-	-	+	-	-	-	2
Type Verbs	+	+	-	+	-	-	+	+	+	+	7
Token Adverbs	-	-	-	-	-	-	-	-	-	-	0
Type Adverbs	-	-	-	+	-	-	+	-	-	-	2
Token Adjectives	+	+	—	+	-	-	+	-	-	-	4
Type Adjectives	+	+	-	+	-	-	+	-	-	+	5
Total number of x̄ scores above median	7	6	1	4	0	1	8	1	3	2	

39

| | High Communication Index | | | | | | Low Communication Index | | | | | | Total x̄ Score above Median |
| | High V.A. | | Med.V.A. | | Low V.A. | | High V.A. | | Med.V.A. | | Low V.A. | | |
	Boys	Girls	Boys	Girls	Boys	Girls	Boys	Girls	Boys	Girls	Boys	Girls	
Total Task Speech	-	+	+	-	-	-	-	-	-	-	+	-	3
Token Nouns	-	-	-	+	-	-	-	-	-	-	-	-	1
Type Nouns	-	-	-	-	-	-	-	-	-	-	-	-	0
Token Verbs	-	-	+	+	-	-	-	-	-	+	+	-	4
Type Verbs	+	+	+	-	-	-	-	-	-	+	+	-	5
Token Adverbs	-	-	+	-	+	-	-	-	-	-	+	-	3
Type Adverbs	-	+	+	+	+	-	+	-	-	-	+	-	6
Token Adjectives	-	-	-	+	-	-	-	+	-	+	-	-	3
Type Adjectives	-	-	-	-	-	-	-	-	-	+	-	-	1
Total number of x̄ scores above median	1	3	5	4	2	0	1	1	0	4	5	0	

It is possible for any one cell to have a total maximum score of nine. We can now make a number of comparisons in the terms of the number of pluses obtained by different sub-groups within the sample. We can also take a closer look at the various sub-group scores on particular measures. We carried out this test despite its crudeness in order to see whether certain of the sub-groups showed a tendency towards consistently higher or lower scores on most of the measures. At the same time, the test makes it possible to examine differences on the various measures when all 22 cells are included in the analysis. First, we shall see whether particular sub-groups of children show consistently high scores across the nine measures, and then we shall examine whether certain sub-groups show a tendency towards high scores on particular form-classes.

(a) Social Class and Verbal Ability

Middle class children of high verbal ability score higher on most of the measures than any of the other sub-groups. The four cells which comprise this group obtained a score of 22 out of a possible 40. The four cells which comprise the group of working class children of High verbal ability produced a total overall score of 6 out of a possible 40.

It is of interest to note that the highest-scoring working class sub-group is the medium ability sub-group who obtain a total overall score of 13.

40

Indeed, this class/ability sub-group obtained a higher score than its middle class counterpart who produced a score of only 10.

(b) Social Class and Communication Index
Although the overall scores of children of High verbal ability appear to be unaffected by their mothers' Communication Index rating, there are two interesting exceptions. Middle class girls' scores are dramatically affected when their mothers' Communication Index scores are *low*. High Communication Index middle class girls of High ability have a score of 6 out of a possible 9 whilst Low Communication Index middle class girls of similar ability obtained a score of only 1 out of a possible 9*. In the working class, the sub-group which is most affected by a Low Communication Index rating is the sub-group of medium verbal ability boys. These children received a score of 0 whilst their High Communication Index comparison group obtained a score of 5. There is also a very slight suggestion that in the working class Low verbal ability sub-group the children with Low Communication Index mothers obtain somewhat higher scores (5) than children with High Communication Index mothers who obtain a score of 2.

(c) Social Class and Type Nouns and Type Adjectives
There is a marked tendency for middle class children to use more nouns and adjectives than working class children. However, we thought that a more critical comparison would be to examine the combined scores of the two class groups in their use of type nouns and type adjectives. This gave a total score of 9 mean scores above the median for the middle class children and one mean score above the median for working class children. A chi-square test for the significance of this difference was carried out. The result indicates that this difference is significant beyond the .01 level ($x^2 = 8.82$ with 1 degree of freedom). This movement within the middle class towards a greater use of type nouns and type adjectives is most marked in the case of High ability children.

One final point should be made. It is possible that there are some inter-correlations between the nine measures but the difference in the summed scores above the median between middle class children and working class children is indeed striking. The sign test revealed association between the overall form-class scores and the communication index score of the mothers and in this way added to the results of the analysis of variance.

We should now consider a number of factors which limit the reliability of the findings.

*It should be noted that middle-class girls of Medium verbal ability are also affected by their mother's Communication Index scores: High Communication Index girls have a higher overall score than Low Communication Index girls (see Table 5).

41

1 The Independent Variables

The statistical description of the Social Class Index and the Communication Index is given in the appendix by Mr. W. Brandis. It is sufficient to note that considerable care was taken over the construction of both the Social Class and Communication Indices. To our knowledge, the construction of the Social Class Index is the only one in this country which is based on a detailed correlational analysis of the component items. The reliability of the Communication Index depends upon whether similar results would be obtained if the schedules upon which it is based were given to the mothers again, as well as upon the statistic used in its construction. The validity of the Index depends upon the truth of the mother's responses. There is no direct means of assessing this, but it is important to note the correlations between the Communication Index scores and other maternal behaviour, and correlations between the Communication Index and the behaviour of the child. (See later chapter.)

Ability tests given to five-year-old children are notoriously unreliable and have little or no predictive value. However, the Crichton Vocabulary Scale was given twice to a group of 18 children. The reliability coefficient after a period of 2 weeks was .88. The correlation between the Crichton Vocabulary Scale scores for the working class sample and their W.I.S.C. scores at six is .538. In this study we were concerned *only* to establish three broad groups of High, Medium and Low ability children according to the distribution of the scores within the sample.

2 The Speech Sample

The amount of speech obtained from each child was relatively small and is distributed across three different tasks. This raises the question of the reliability of the scores obtained from such a small yet differentiated sample of speech. However, the fact that the children were barely five years old and had been at school only three weeks, must be taken into account. To have increased the speech sample would have meant increasing the testing time well beyond half an hour and so would have increased the possibility of fatigue for the children. Alternatively, to have tested each child twice would have added enormously to the cost of the speech collection and would have placed additional burdens on the schools. It should be remembered that during this period the children were also given three ability tests.

The Unit decided that it was more important to offer the children a variety of contexts rather than to offer one context to explore in depth, because it was considered that the grammar and lexes produced would be closely related to the context. Therefore the speech schedule was concerned with the child's ability to develop speech appropriate to different contexts.* A future Unit monograph will be concerned with the

*The contextual dependence of the children's form class usage will be examined in Part 2 of this paper.

examination of differences in the grammar used on each task. As the children were also given the speech schedule when they were seven years of age it is possible to undertake an analysis of changes in the grammar and lexes between five and seven in relation to specific tasks. Thus the Unit deliberately chose to offer the children a variety of contexts although there was a risk of reducing the amount of speech for each task. We thought that the sample size was large enough to compensate for the reduced amount of speech obtained from each child.

3 Variance within Form-Class Usage

One of the major problems in the analysis of speech obtained from the children is the large variation observed between individual children in both the frequency of grammatical elements and in the frequency of form-class usage. Although in principle, it is possible to estimate the size of sample required in order to allow for this variation, it is quite likely that the sample size required would make research extremely costly. It is therefore important to bear in mind that the differences obtained between social class groups masks considerable variation between the children in each social class (see Appendix for Analyses of Variance).

4 The Tasks

The speech schedule was piloted upon 20 middle class and 20 working class children, before it was given to the research sample of children. However, our experience is such that we would recommend that all research into language should begin with an extensive period of piloting of the material despite the increase in the cost of the research.

The design of a speech schedule which would be equally interesting and testing to children of a wide range of ability who span the social class range is an intractable problem. The only evidence available which suggests that the tasks were of similar interest to the children is the finding that there was no significant difference in the amount of task-relevant speech offered by the two social classes. It should be pointed out that this is a very crude index of the significance of the tasks for the various class and ability groups. It is also important to consider the relative attractiveness of the tasks to five-year-old boys and girls. Whilst it is true that the sex of the child had a bearing upon his or her form-class scores, we are unable to determine whether this reflects a basic difference between the sexes in their linguistic behaviour or whether this is because the inter-personal nature of the Picture Story Cards and the Trotin Cards was more stimulating to girls rather than boys. It is interesting to speculate on the possibility of a reversal of these sex differences if the children had been asked to build a model railway and talk about that.

5 The Collection of the Speech

The conditions under which the speech was collected varied from school

43

to school. All schools did all that they could to provide a room in which to interview each child but clearly many of the schools had major problems of accommodation. The conditions in some schools were therefore not as favourable as in others. The rooms available varied in size from the very large to the very small, and they also varied in noise-level. In one middle class school the overcrowding was such that the head and staff very kindly put their staff-room at the disposal of the Unit. It is also the case that the speech obtained may well have been influenced by differences in the initial responses of children to school life. Some children settle down quickly, whilst others may need a whole term at school (Plowden Report). It was very important to obtain the speech from the children before the school and teaching produced possible linguistic effects, and there was therefore no alternative but to collect the speech at the beginning of the child's life at school.

Each interviewer however, spent a day in the classroom before the children were interviewed, so that the children could become familiar with her.

6 The Interviewers
Over 300 children in the working class area were given the speech schedule. Five women interviewers were responsible for the collection of the speech. Three of the interviewers were researchers of the Unit and two were part-time members. The two part-time workers had taught in infant schools. Differences in personality between interviewers, and variations between interviewers in the way they presented the speech schedule were also a source of unreliability. It is difficult to see how such a sample could have been collected within the time period without employing a large number of interviewers. The middle class sample of 150 five-year-old children was collected *one* year later. A Ford Foundation grant made it possible to extend the research to a middle class area. Four women interviewers interviewed the middle class children, two of whom had collected speech from the working class children. There was less deviation from the schedule during the collection of speech in the middle class area, and minimal extra reinforcements were given. It is thus possible that the working class children found the interview situation warmer and more relaxed than did the middle class children.

7 The Factorial Design
The factorial design allowed for the matching of the children upon a range of variables which makes this particular research unusual in language studies. However, the degree of matching on each of the variables varies. The matching for Medium and Low verbal ability for each social class is particularly poor, but it should be stressed that this does not invalidate the results since the main verbal ability effects are related to the High verbal ability group, where the matching of High verbal ability groups who differ

in social class is clearly acceptable. The composition of the middle class sample was such that it may have tended to reduce the chances of differences when a comparison was made between the social class groups. The middle class sample contained ten children whose parents were assigned marginal middle class status in terms of the Unit's Index of Social Class. The simple dichotomy of the maternal Communication Index scores reduced the effect of this variable as it was not possible to compare extreme scores. It should be borne in mind that the Unit has since developed a more complex index of maternal communication and control but this index could not be used as it was developed *after* the factorial design was set up. Finally, it should be emphasised that it is not possible to generalise from the findings revealed through this factorial design to the rest of the middle class and working class research sample. The distribution of the defining variables in the parent sample is different from their distribution in the factorial sample. The results which are presented have, therefore, only internal validity.

8 Comparability of Criteria

This point refers to comparability with other studies rather than reliability. The scores obtained in each of the form-classes related to their defining criteria. It is important that minimal definitions should be agreed in order that future studies can be made comparable. Clearly, specific research problems set up their own particular demands upon the definition of categories selected for analysis, but it should still be possible to develop a minimum set of definitions of selected categories. Perhaps, of most importance, is the need for some standardisation of the contexts used for obtaining speech. It may well be that more research is required in order that a range of contexts can be designed which will enable children of different sex and ability to show the various ways in which they are able to explore the uses of language.

A number of language studies have been undertaken in an attempt to determine the importance of particular environmental factors in vocabulary development. Various studies of cognitive development have offered results which indicate that the presence of a verbal label facilitates performance on some cognitive tasks. Unfortunately, it is not possible to review these findings fully in this paper, but a number of relevant studies are included in the bibliography at the end of this chapter.

Discussion of Results

Introduction

Before the results are discussed, an important qualification must be made. Thirty-three analyses of variance were carried out on the data, and it is probable that a number of significant differences could have arisen by

45

chance. We have decided to ignore differences at the 5% level in the discussion of the results. However, attention will be directed to the recurring *pattern* of the interaction between social class and verbal ability scores, although the level of significance of this interaction is only at the 5% level.

We shall refer in this discussion to a set of choices within a system which in Halliday's Scale and Category Grammar is called the nominal group. G. Turner writes 'Halliday. . . . . .has indicated that to a large extent the early conceptual structure of the child is determined by the choices available in the nominal group. . . . . . Moreover, the nominal group normally operates in clause structure, and one of its chief functions there is to associate participants. . . . . with a process and to state, as required, particular attributes and circumstances of the process and participators'. The principal elements in the nominal group are a modifier (M), a head (H) and a qualifier (Q). Only the head is an obligatory element, the modifier and qualifier are optional elements. We give below some examples of the nominal group.

	N.G.		N.G.	
1.	The doll's got		yellow hair	
	M	H	M	H

	N.G.		N.G.		
2.	Pretty dolly's got		short yellow hair		
	M	H	M	M	H

	N.G.		N.G.			
3.	Pretty dolly's got		short yellow hair with a bow			
	M	H	M	M	H	Q

	N.G.	N.G.
4.	Pretty dolly	is naughty

The above is only a very crude description of the choices within the nominal group system. For a more precise and delicate analysis the reader is referred to the Sociological Research Unit Monograph 'A Grammatical Analysis and Computer Program for Children's Speech' by Mohan, B. and Turner, G. Hawkins, P. in another monograph 'Social Class and the Nominal Group', will present a most detailed analysis of the influence of social class upon the choices five-year-old children take up within the nominal group. This discussion is concerned only with what are called the open set lexical choices within the nominal group. The open set lexical choices are the nouns and adjectives.

We were interested in the nominal group because its elements control the verbal realisation of categories, the ascription of attributes to categories and their further elaboration.

We shall discuss the results as these relate to the social class position of the parents, to the ability level of the child, to the mother's score on the Communication Index, and, finally, as they relate to the sex of the child.

Social Class

Middle class children, particularly those of high verbal ability, used more token nouns, more type nouns and more type adjectives than did working class children. Middle class children, irrespective of verbal ability, also used more type verbs.

Now, it is unlikely that working class children do not possess in their passive vocabulary the middle class range of adjectival, noun and verb-types used in the tasks. It is even more unlikely that middle class and working class children differ in terms of their tacit understanding of the linguistic rule system. Therefore we are faced with the problem of the sub-cultural influences acting through the family relationships sensitising one group of children towards greater verbal differentiation and to the offering of their experience in a more explicit and individuated way. This should not be taken to mean that the speech of working class children does not possess its own aesthetic, nor that their imagination is not verbally realised. It is more the case that there is a difference in the social function of language (Bernstein 1964).

The middle class children show a greater preference for taking up open-set choices (nouns and adjectives) within the nominal group. This points to a greater concern with making explicit the classification and differentiation of persons, states and objects, together with a greater specificity in the ascription of attributes. For example, middle class children are more likely to say 'The people are having a meal' than 'They're eating', and these children are more likely than working class children to extend this statement to 'The people are having a nice meal'. Middle class children, then, in terms of our findings, are much more likely to make the class-naming principle verbally explicit and make fuller distinctions within each class through the ascription of specific attributes.

Our analysis did not attempt to distinguish between types of nouns or types of adjectives, nor did we try to show differential preferences between types of nouns most likely to be qualified. Future Unit work will be concerned with such possible differences.

If the middle class children were moving towards the choices within the nominal group, then there is some indication that the working class were more likely to take up adverbial choices. This finding appears twice. Firstly, in the t-test, when we compared the total middle class sample with the total working class sample. Secondly, the sign test shows that the score above the median for token adverbs and type adverbs for the middle class groups is 2 whereas the score for the total working class group is 9. The impression we have, and Geoffrey Turner's work would seem to confirm this, is that the working class children are more concerned with adverbs of location, 'up', 'down', 'there', 'out', than with adverbs of manner, 'slowly', 'quickly'. It is tempting to suggest this *relative* preference shows a concern with bounding an action/process in space rather than a concern with the *way* a person or object manifests itself. We must again emphasise that there is no reason for believing that adverbs of manner are not in the lexes of working class children. In fact they are, and every teacher is witness to this. All that we can say is that when working class and middle class children are presented with similar tasks, but undoubtedly different *social* contexts, the options taken up by the working class children differ markedly from the options taken up by middle class children. Whilst it might be argued that the lack of differentiation in the working class children's lexes has to do with sub-cultural constraints upon the speech of the child in the interview situation, it is not easy to understand why interacting with an adult should encourage the working class child's preference for adverbs of location.

Ability
There are difficulties in interpreting the findings which are associated with ability. In the first place we cannot place much reliance upon the scores obtained from young children and this comment holds especially for the low scoring children. The Crichton test is scored in such a way that if a low scoring child obtained one or two more accurate definitions he would be placed in the average range. Secondly, low scores on the part of working class children tells us more about the environment of the child than they tell us about the child himself. Thirdly, although we made an attempt to match middle class and working class children at three levels of ability, the social significance of these ability levels varies with the social class groups. For example, where an average ability score is typical within working class groups an average ability score is much less typical within middle class groups. In other words, a middle class child of average ability is under stresses quite different from a working class child of average ability. This point probably holds more when children of below average are compared. Thus the speech of a middle class five-year-old child of average ability may well be less differentiated because of the pressures placed upon him at home where he may be more talked at and this might lead to a more passive interview relation. Whereas a working class child of average ability may be less pressurised and possibly less passive in relationships with adults where he is expected to be active.

These qualifications may help us to understand the ability findings.

Whilst it is the case that the main order analysis of variance persistently showed that the middle class children obtained higher scores on token nouns, different nouns and different adjectives, it is also the case that there was a recurring interaction effect between social class and verbal ability. These interaction effects reveal that middle class children show particularly high scores on these measures when their verbal ability scores are high. We did not find such interaction effects for token nouns, different nouns and different adjectives in the case of the working class sample. Indeed, within the working class sample there is a hint that the scores of Medium ability working class children are somewhat higher than the scores of working class children of High ability. We do not know whether the possession of High ability is responsible for the readiness with which middle class children take up the open set options within the nominal group, or whether this readiness is related to differences within the middle class in the socialisation of High and Medium ability children. There is a suggestion in a forthcoming Research Unit monograph on 'Social Class and the Infant School Child' by Jean Jones that middle class children of Low ability are socialised into a more passive role than middle class children of High ability.

Within the working class we are faced with the depression of the scores of High ability children. Wiseman (1964) has argued that children of High ability are most sensitive to their environment. Therefore we might expect the great difference between the High ability working class children and the High ability middle class children. It might also be that bright five-year-old working class children are more concerned with and take a leading part in the activities of their peer group. This would tend to restrict their verbal development because of the nature of the activities and the continuous presence of other children as speech models.

A puzzling finding is the higher scores of Medium ability children when compared with High ability children on type adverbs. Earlier we reported a move towards the nominal group on the part of middle class children and a move towards the adverb on the part of the working class children. It is possible that the higher scores on type adverbs obtained by the Medium ability children arises out of their greater use of locational adverbs. This in turn would reflect how they structured the picture stories and Trotin cards.

Before leaving this section we might consider whether it is appropriate to create the same tasks for all ability groups and then to compare the performance of the less able children with the performance of the more able. Perhaps we should scale the tasks in accordance with the different ability ranges and then compare the effects of different social backgrounds upon the children's performance. It should also be borne in mind that our study is concerned with encoding (speech production) not with decoding (comprehension). Thus differences in speech production may or may not parallel differences in comprehension. The relationship between speech production and comprehension may be different for the different ability ranges *and* affected by the cultural background of the children.

The Communication Index

This measure of the mother's reported communications to her child provided us with some interesting findings. In as much as there are relationships between this measure and the speech of the children then we can have some confidence in the reports of the mothers of what they say they do. We should note that sub-sample 2 of the main analysis compared working and middle class children whose mothers scored high on the Communication Index. Thus the score on the Communication Index was the major independent variable in this comparison. When we compared the results of this comparison with the results of the comparison made in sub-sample 1 (which contained two ability ranges and High and Low Maternal Communication Index scores) we found that, holding the Communication Index constant, the number of significant differences on the children's form class scores were markedly reduced. The significant social class differences found in the use of type verbs, token verbs and token adverbs disappeared. The social class difference in the open-set choices within the nominal group (token nouns, type nouns and type adjectives) remained. It would seem then in terms of our limited analysis that High Maternal Communication scores *within* the working class narrows differences between the social classes as these occur in the area of the verbal and adverbial group. Does this mean that communicating mothers within the working class develop in their children a greater sensitivity towards the linguistic realisation of categories and the ascription of attributes to these categories? This is a matter for further investigation. We should also bear in mind that there was an interaction effect which showed that working class children, particularly those of Medium ability with High communicating mothers used more token verbs than middle class children.

We also found that there was a general trend for Low Maternal Index scores to be associated with a greater use of token verbs particularly with the use of the verb 'to be'. We should remember that differences found when the token verb count was analysed disappeared when the verb 'to be' was omitted from the count. We decided that the use of the verb 'to be' was a function of listing behaviour on the part of the children, e.g. 'That's a man, there's a house'. Listing behaviour is to be expected in five-year-old children and, indeed one of the tasks, the Trotin Cards, clearly encouraged listing behaviour. It is therefore no surprise to find such behaviour related to all the variables. However it is the case that children of mothers with Low Communication Index scores listed more than the children of mothers with High Communication Index scores. When we analysed this finding in greater detail we found that the children most inclined to list were middle class *boys* whose mothers obtained a low score on the Communication Index. Thus it would seem that in the middle class Low communicating mothers reduce elaboration in the children's speech as this is indexed by listing behaviour.

We were interested in the fact that significant differences in the frequency with which the verb 'to be' was used were *not* found when comparisons were made *within* the High Communication Index sub-sample. In view of the fact that listing may imply an increased use of nouns, e.g. 'There's a man, there's a train, there's a guard', one would perhaps have expected that the analysis of noun usage would also reveal a relationship between social class and the Communication Index ratings of the children's mothers. This relationship was not found and we offer a possible explanation. It may be that middle class children with High Communication Index mothers are likely to use a high proportion of nouns in relation to the verb 'to be' in each clause or sentence, e.g. 'That man in the train is a guard'. Whereas middle class children, especially boys with Low Communication Index mothers, use a *lower* proportion of nouns in relation to the verb 'to be' in each clause or sentence, e.g. 'That's a man. . . . . He's a guard' 'There's his train'. In both cases the *number* of nouns is the same and therefore no significant interaction effect between social class would be revealed in an analysis of noun usage. This finding suggests that middle class boys with Low Communication Index mothers may have a tendency to offer short simple sentences in which the verb 'to be' is used as a pointer. Within the middle class it looks as if the boys with Low Communication Index mothers are more likely to reduce the verbal elaboration of relationships. This would be in accordance with their mother's reports that they explained less to their children and were less likely to take up the children's attempts to initiate conversation.

It is clear that these differences cannot be attributed to differences in the measured ability of the middle class children. These differences are in some way connected with the consequences, for the children, of differences in the Communication Index score of the mothers.

Without doubt the most interesting finding associated with the Communication Index is its effect upon the form class scores of middle class girls. We found, on the whole, few sex differences in the form class scores of the middle class children but this was because we did not take into account the startling affect upon the girls' form class scores of the mothers' Maternal Index score. The sign test revealed that middle class girls whose mothers scored high on this Index received a score of ten for their form class scores which were above the median for the total sample, whilst middle class girls whose mothers scored low on the Index received a score of only three. This discrepancy is most marked for girls of High verbal ability, where such girls of Low communicating mothers obtain a score of only one, whereas the girls of High communicating mothers obtain a score of six. We find, then, that the reduced sex differences in form class scores within the middle class is because half the girls scored low and half the girls scored high. Indeed when we look at the raw scores of the girls with High communicating mothers these scores tended to be higher than the raw scores of middle class boys with High communicating mothers.

Our research has also revealed (see Bernstein and Brandis) that the middle class mothers tend to be more coercive towards the girl rather than to the boy and they are less ready to give explanations to the girl. These sex differences in patterns of communication and control were not found within the working class sample. Bernstein and Brandis suggest that there is a tendency within the middle class to socialise the girl into a more submissive social role than that of the boy. It is possible, then, that the middle class girl's form class differentiation is related to the mothers' pattern of communication and control. Whilst maturational differences between boys and girls may affect their use of language it does appear that the familial shaping of children's social roles is also an important influence. We shall refer to this point again in the following section.

There is one further relationship between the Communication Index score of the mother and the speech of the children. The sign test suggested that *within* the working class, holding Medium ability of the children constant, the form class differentiation of *boys* with mothers who scored high on the Communication Index is greater than that of the *boys* whose mothers obtained a low score on the Communication Index. There are five scores above the medium for the whole sample in the former case and *no* scores above the medium in the latter case. The scores are on token verbs, type verbs, token adverbs and type adverbs. We should also remember that there is some suggestion in the sign test that Medium ability working class children have higher scores than High ability working class children across verbs and adverbs. Does a high score on the Maternal Communication Index in the case of working class boys of Medium ability give an added impetus towards the verb and adverb which is perhaps already an orientation of the early linguistic socialisation? And if so, why is it a ability specific? We can only raise these questions and hope that the picture will become clearer when a much larger sample of children's speech has been analysed. At the moment we must be cautious indeed, about the interpretation of this finding.

In general the Communication Index acts to reduce differences between the working class and middle class sample; it is associated with listing behaviour, particularly so in the case of middle class boys; it is associated with depressed form class scores obtained by middle class girls; it is associated with a greater move towards the verb and adverb on the part of working class boys of Medium ability.

Sex

A significant main order sex difference, which was unaffected by any of the interaction analyses occurred in the use of different adjectives. This suggests that five-year-old girls, irrespective of social class, are more likely to assign attributes than are boys. This difference between boys and girls is greater within the working class sample. Further the sign test revealed that in the case of the working class sample there were only *five* scores in the area of token nouns, type nouns, token adjectives, type adjectives that were above the median scores for the total sample of these form classes. These five scores above the median were *all* obtained by the working class girls. There is no difference in the middle class sample between boys and girls who scored above the median in the noun and adjectival area.

Bernstein (1968) has suggested that within working class families, especially large families, we can expect a marked difference between boys and girls in their use of language. These differences may well arise out of differences in their social roles. Older girls in working class families tend to take on mothering roles combined with a mediating role between parents and siblings. Thus the social role of older girls is more complex as it incorporates a normal sibling role with one of mediator and one of controller. Girls are likely to have to rely upon forms of control based rather more upon linguistically elaborated meanings than upon physical coercion. They are placed in situations involving a variety of role and speech variant switching, e.g. girl – girl, girl – boy, girl controlling girl, girl controlling boy, girl mediating between parents and siblings. Further girls are less tied to an activity dominated peer group structure than boys. The relative isolation from such a structure, combined with their more complex role-set is likely to develop the girl's orientation towards a more differentiated, more individuated use of language in inter-personal contexts. The older working class girl is likely to serve as a language model for younger girls in the family. It is very possible that the large sex differences in the use of adjectives and a move towards the noun within the working class sample, maybe a reflection of the fact that the language and social role models of the working class girls are older girl siblings. It is not possible to test this hypothesis, which relates the orientation to language use to the learning of social roles in our limited sample.

It is interesting to note that the largest sex differences in the ascription of attributes (use of adjectives) within the middle class occurs between boys and girls of High verbal ability but the sex difference in the use of adjectives in the working class is *not* related to ability. This finding is some support for the social role argument.

It has been suggested that an optimum environment for *certain* uses of language can be equated with a middle class environment and that this environment is more conducive than a working class environment for the development of choices within the nominal group. It seems that, whatever the role of maturational factors, there is a differential movement towards the noun/adjectival choices on the part of middle class girls whose mothers differ in their Communication Index ratings. If there is a maturational factor which affects these choices then such choices are given an increased impetus where the process of communication to the middle class girl is more elaborated. On the other hand lexical differentiation within the nominal group, according to our findings will develop in the middle class boy *irrespective* of the mother's measure of reported communication. It

53

may be that the content of a low score on the Communication Index (what is actually said), in relation to a middle class boy maybe very different from what is actually said by a low scoring middle class mother to a girl. It, of course, may well be the case, that the middle class boy's general cultural environment is more stimulating than that of the girl except in the case where the girl's mother is verbally elaborating their relationship.

Our findings suggest social factors at work which orient the working class girl towards the open set choices within the nominal group and which affect the form class differentiation of the middle class girl. We have suggested that these differences reflect differences in social role learning.

Conclusion

We have interpreted the broad differences between the children as representing a movement in the middle class children towards exploring the choice system with the nominal group. We should point out that a detailed grammatical analysis of this group and its implication will be given by Hawkins in a forthcoming Research Unit monograph. We have concerned ourselves only with the open set lexical choices. We have further suggested the possibility that if the middle class children are moving towards the nominal group then we might tentatively suggest that the working class children are moving towards the verb/adverb area, in terms of their verbal realisation of the three tasks used for this analysis. The data we have presented is an inadequate basis for speculation about the sub-cultural influences upon orientation towards different uses of language. However, it raises this question.

We shall consider very briefly the possible significance of the middle class children's movement towards the nominal group without prejudice to Hawkins' much more delicate study.

Young children are less able to develop the possibilities of the language at sentence and clause rank but the early development of the nominal group may well develop the integration of the nominal group into the clause structure as the children get older. In other words, the middle class children's greater emphasis on the development within the nominal group at five years of age may increase their chances of producing a more developed and flexible clause structure later. At the semantic level, there is likely to be a dynamic reverberation of meanings (arising out of the inter-connections) across the greater differentiation of their verbally realised classifications. This may well have consequences for conceptual development. However, it should be pointed out that the relationship between having the label and having the concept is not necessarily one to one. It may be a little unwise to link the exploration of the nominal group with a *general* cognitive advantage. What is required is an enquiry into the *specific* cognitive implications of early development of the nominal group.

One advantage of this movement may be its effect upon verbal ability scores.

An analysis carried out by W. Brandis indicates that there is a clear relationship between high social class position of the parents, and children who score higher on the vocabulary scale than on the similarity scale of the W.I.S.C. Whatever the general cognitive implications are of early development of the nominal group it is certainly the case that middle class children stand a very, very much better chance of obtaining higher I.Q. scores than do working class children on tests such as the W.I.S.C.

On the whole the Maternal Communication Index produced rather more dramatic findings within the middle class than within the working class. In the following section by Bernstein and Brandis, this matter will be taken up in the light of a discussion of a greater number of variables.

It is important to point out that these social class differences in the children's use of language arose out of a particular social context and out of very specific tasks. Whilst it is true that the results indicate that the sub-cultural shaping of family relationships within the middle class encourages these children to develop certain areas of language which are important for their school experience we must emphasise that every culture and sub-culture carries its own aesthetic and its own unique, imaginative potential.

Finally, we should alert the reader to the fact that more detailed analyses of the children's speech may well modify or confirm the conclusion reached in this limited analysis of the open set lexical choices within the nominal group. This caution applies particularly to the statements in the discussion which refer to the working class children's verb/adverbial choices.

Conclusions

The analysis of form-class usage revealed the following results:
1 Middle class children, particularly those of High verbal ability, used more token nouns, more type nouns and more type adjectives than working class children. Middle class children also used more type verbs than working class children, irrespective of verbal ability.
2 Working class children, particularly those of Medium verbal ability whose mothers have High Maternal Communication Index ratings, used more token adverbs than middle class children. We have reason to believe, from results of the grammatical analysis of the children's speech, that these are mainly locational adverbs.
3 Girls used more token adjectives and more type adjectives than boys. This sex difference in the use of these form-classes was greater in the working class than in the middle class.
4 Medium verbal ability children used more type adverbs than High verbal ability children.

5 Middle class girls, particularly those of High verbal ability, whose mothers have Low Maternal Communication Index ratings showed an overall depression of their form-class scores compared to middle class girls whose mothers have High Maternal Communication Index ratings.

6 Middle class boys whose mothers have Low Maternal Communication Index ratings used more token verbs than middle class boys whose mothers have High Maternal Communication Index ratings. High scores on token verbs were found to be almost wholly dependent upon the frequency with which these boys used the verb 'to be'. This indicates that middle class boys whose mothers have Low Maternal Communication Index ratings show simple listing behaviour to a greater extent than middle class boys whose mothers have High Maternal Communication Index ratings.

We have interpreted the above findings in terms of a greater emphasis upon the linguistic categorising and elaborating of relations within the middle class. We have suggested that the *overall* findings indicate that the middle-class children, relative to the working class, are more likely to take up options within the nominal group, whereas working-class children, especially boys, have a tendency towards the verb/adverb. We have also suggested that the type of social role learned by the child influences form-class usage.

REFERENCES

Bernstein, B. (1961) Social Class and Linguistic Development: a theory of social learning, in *Education. Economy and Society* (Eds.) Halsey, A. H., Floud J. and Anderson, C. A. (New York)

Bernstein, B. (1962a) Social Class, Linguistic Codes and Grammatical Elements, *Language and Speech*, 5

Bernstein, B. (1962b) Linguistic Codes, Hesitation Phenomena and Intelligence, *Language and Speech*, 5

Bernstein, B. (1964) Elaborated and Restricted Codes: their social origins and some consequences in Gumperz, J. and Hymes, D. (Eds.) *The Ethnography of Communication*, American Anthropologist Special Publication, 66, No.6, Part 2. [Reprinted in Smith, A. G. (Ed.) *Communication and Culture*, New York: Holt, Rinehart and Winston, 1966]

Bossard, J. H. S. (1948) Family modes of expression in Bossard, J. H. S. *The Sociology of Child Development*, Ch.9, New York: Harper & Brothers

Brown, R. W. (1965) Language: The System and its Acquisition in Brown, R. *Social Psychology*, Chs.6 & 7, New York: The Free Press

Carrol, J. B. (1938) Diversity of vocabulary and harmonic series of word frequency distribution, *Psychological Record*, 2

Cazden, C. B. (1966) Subcultural differences in child language: an interdisciplinary review, *Merrill Palmer Quarterly*, 12

Deutsch, M. (1963) The disadvantaged child and the learning process, in Passow, A. H. (Ed.), *Education in depressed areas*, New York: Columbia University.

Deutsch, M. (1965) The role of social class in language development and cognition, *American Journal of Orthopsychiatry*, 25

Goodenough, F. L. (1938) The use of pronouns by young children: a note on the development of selfawareness. *Journal of Genetic Psychology*, 52

Halliday, M. (1966) *Grammar, Society and the Noun,* An Inaugural Lecture delivered at University College, London

Hess, R. D. & Shipman, V. (1965a) Early experience and the socialisation of cognitive modes in children, *Child Development*, 36

Hess, R. D. & Shipman, V. (1965b) Early blocks to children's learning, *Children*, 12

Irwin, O. C. (1948a) Infant speech: the effect of family occupational status and of age on use of sound types, *Journal of Speech and Hearing Disorders*, 13

Irwin, O. C. (1948b) Infant speech: the effect of family occupational status and of age on sound frequency, *Journal of Speech and Hearing Disorders*, 13

John, V. (1963) The intellectual development of slum children: some preliminary findings, *American Journal of Orthopsychiatry*, 33

John V. & Goldstein, L. (1964) The social context of language acquisition, *Merrill Palmer Quarterly*, 10

Khater, M. R. (1951) The influence of social class on the language patterns of kindergarten children, Unpublished doctoral dissertation, University of Chicago.

Lawton, D. (1963) Social class language differences in language development: a study of some samples of written work, *Language and Speech*, 6

Lawton, D. (1964) Social class language differences in group discussions, *Language and Speech*, 7

Loban, W. (1963) *The Language of elementary school children*, N.C.T.E. Research Report No. 1 Champaign, Illinois.

Loban, W. (1965) Language proficiency and school learning, in Krumboltz, J. D. (Ed.), *Learning and the educational process*, Chicago: Rand McNally.

Luria, A. R. & Yudovich, I. (1959) *Speech and the Development of Mental Processes in the Child*, London.

Marge, M. (1965) The influence of selected home background variables on the development of oral communication skills in children, *Journal of Speech and Hearing Research*, 8

McCarthy, D. M. (1965) Language Development in Children, in Carmichael, L. (Ed.) *Manual of Child Psychology*

Milner, E. (1951) A study of the relationship between reading readiness in grade one school-children and patterns of parent-child interaction, Child Development, 22

Moore, J. K. (1947) Speech content of selected groups of orphanage and non-orphanage pre-school children. *Journal of Experimental Education*, 16

Pyles, M. K. (1932) Verbalisation as a factor in learning, *Child Development*, 3

Robinson, W. P. (1965a), Cloze procedure as a technique for the investigation of social class differences in language usage. *Language and Speech*, 8

Robinson, W. P. (1965b) The elaborated code in working class language, *Language and Speech*, 8

Sampson, O. C. (1959) The speech and language development of 5 year old children. *British Journal of Educational Psychology*, 29

Schatzman, L. & Strauss, A. (1955) Social class and modes of communication, *American Journal of Sociology*, 60 (Reprinted in Smith, A. G. (Ed.)) *Communication and culture*, New York: Holt, Rinehart and Winston, 1966

Shepard, W. O. & Schaffer, M. (1956) The effect of concept knowledge on discriminating learning, *Child Development*, 27

Smith, M. E. (1926) An investigation of the development of the sentence and the extent of vocabulary in young children. *University of Iowa Study of Child Welfare*, 3 No. 5

Spiker, L., Gerynoy, J. R. & Shepard, W. O. (1956) Children's concepts of middle-sizedness and performance of the intermediate size problem, *Journal of Occupational Psychology*, 79

Strickland, R. (1962) The language of elementary school children. *Bulletin of School of Education*, Vol. 38, No.4

Templin, M. C. (1957) Certain language skills in children, *Institute of Child Welfare Monograph*, No.26

Templin, M. C. (1958) Relation of speech and language development to intelligence and socio-economic status, *Volta Review*, 60

Weir, M. W. & Stephensen, H. W. (1959) The effects of verbalisation in children's learning, *Child Development*, 30

Williams, H. M. & McFarland, M. L.(1937) The development of language and vocabulary in young children, *University of Iowa Study of Child Welfare*, 13, No.2

Wiseman, S. (1964) *Education and Environment*, Manchester University Press

Wiseman, S. (1967) *Children and their Primary Schools,* A report of the Central Advisory Council for Education (England), Vol.2

APPENDIX

CRITERIA FOR IDENTIFYING THE FORM-CLASSES

Since the aim of the analysis was to isolate those places in the structure of the language where there is clearly occurring selection from a wide range of possibilities, only those choices which are clearly open-set choices were examined. It was essential that the methods of classification should be as straightforward and non-technical as possible. To this end we decided to make use of the test frames given by Fries (The Structure of English, 1952). He uses the test frames to set up what he calls 'form-classes' or parts of speech. He isolates four classes of words: Class 1, Class 2, Class 3 and Class 4. These classes correspond very largely to the traditional word-classes: nouns, verbs, adjectives and adverbs. In our exposition we have used the traditional terms in preference to Fries' terms, but it must be remembered that Fries' test frames formed the basis of the classification. In a number of places we have added frames and criteria in order to make as explicit as possible the basis on which the classifications were made. For these additional criteria we have drawn on Strang (1961) and on scale-and-category grammar (see, for example, Halliday et al., 1964 and Sinclair, 1965).

In this description of the criteria used for the identification of the form-classes we give first, a brief 'technical' description and second, a 'non-technical' description of the methods of classification.

Nouns

Nouns comply with the following set of criteria:

Technical'
1 They can be the Subject of the Complement of a clause. More strictly, they operate as head-words in nominal groups that can be the Subject or the Complement of a clause. The first blank in Fries' Frames, A, B and C concerns the Subject, and the second blank in Frame B concerns the Complement.
2 They can be Complement to a preposition. More strictly, they operate as head-words in nominal groups that can operate as Complement to a preposition. Fries does not give a test-frame for this position, so we provided one, Frame D.

3 They can directly follow a closed class of items known as 'determiners' for example: *the, a, my*.

4 They usually select in a system a number which has two terms' 'singular' and 'plural', the latter normally being morphologically marked by *-s*.

'Non-technical'

1 May fill at least one of the following blanks:

Frame A

The _____ is/was good.

_____ s are/were good

e.g. concert

Frame B

The _____ remembered the _____.

s   _____ s.

e.g. clerk   tax

Frame C

The _____ went there.

_____ s

e.g. team

Frame D

He looked at the _____.

e.g. scene

2 Often (but not always) follow one of the following words:

the	e.g. the man
a	e.g. a boy
my, your, his, her, its, our, their	e.g. his mother
this, these, that, those	e.g. this car
which, what, whose	e.g. whose ball
some, every, each, any, no, another	e.g. some boys
both, all, some, other, own	e.g. both men

3 Often (but not always) may be either singular or plural. Plural is usually shown by *-s* ending.

e.g. boy, boys

lady, ladies

But also: man, men

child, children

List of Nouns for the Football Picture Story

ball, boy, children, door, football, finger, fist, frown, goal, hole, house, kick, lady, man, policeman, woman, window.

Verbs

'Technical'

1 They can be the Predicator in the structure of the clause. Put more precisely, they operate at the lexical element (the final element) in verbal groups that operate at the Predicator.

2 The verbal group has a number of different systems operating within it, tense, modality, polarity, etc. For two reasons it is possible to make use of our knowledge of these systems for identifying the verb-words: one, some systems determine the ending of the verb-word, and two, all of the systems are realised by words which occur in close proximity to the verb-words. In the 'non-technical' criteria we make particular use of the systems of tense, modality and polarity, mainly as defined by Halliday (1966). Thus, numbers 2 and 3 of the 'non-technical' criteria are to do with tense; number 4 with modality; and number 5 with polarity.

'Non-technical'

1 May fill at least one of the following blanks:

Frame A

The concert _____ good.

Coffee _____ good.

Concerts ___ good.

e.g.   is/was
are/were
seems/seemed

Frame B

The clerk _____ the tax.

e.g.   remembered
wanted

Frame C

The team _____ there.

e.g.   went
came

2 Refer to time:

past	e.g. did take
present	e.g. takes, does take
future	e.g. will take
etc.	e.g. had taken, has taken, will have taken.

3 Often preceded by the following words: (note that the endings are sometimes also given)

did		e.g. did take
does		e.g. does take
will		e.g. will take
had	-ed, -en	e.g. had borrowed, taken
has	-ed, -en	e.g. has borrowed, taken
will have	-ed, -en	e.g. will have borrowed, taken
was	-ing	e.g. was taking
is	-ing	e.g. is taking
will be	-ing	e.g. will be taking
was going to		e.g. was going to take
is going to		e.g. is going to take
will be going to		e.g. will be going to take

4 Occasionally preceded by the following words:

could/can   e.g. he could go
was to/is to
used to
would
should
may
might
must
ought to
got to

5 Occasionally associated with *n't* or *not*

         e.g. he did*n't* catch any fish
              he did *not* catch any fish

6 Can end in *-ed*, *-en*, *-ing*

         e.g. he fished
              it had eaten, it was eaten
              he was fishing

N.B. words with these endings are *not* verbs if they can be preceded by *very* or *quite*.

7 Concerning *be*, *have*, *do* and *go*, we need criteria for distinguishing their lexical use from their grammatical use. As a simple expedient we give the most normal meanings that these words are likely to have when they are used as lexical words in the children's speech.

   (A) *be* (e.g. is, was)

         (i) exist, occur, live

             e.g. There's a man
                  A man is there

        (ii) 'may be described as'

             e.g. He is a man
                  He is good.

        (iii) 'may be identified as'

             e.g. That is the train.

   (B) *have* (e.g. has, had)

         (i) possess, contain

             e.g. The train has three carriages.

        (ii) be obliged

             e.g. I had my work to do.

        (iii) experience something

             e.g. I had my leg broken.

   (C) *do* (e.g. does, did)

         (i) perform, carry out, effect

             e.g. You've done a good job

        (ii) act

             e.g. He did wisely.

(D) *go* (e.g. goes, went)
    (i) start, depart
        e.g. The train went out of the station.
    (ii) continue moving, travel
        e.g. The train was going down the track.

N.B. Concerning *be going to*: if *be about to* is a possible substitute, then do not count it,

e.g. He $\begin{array}{c}\text{is going to}\\\text{is about to}\end{array}$ meet someone.

List of Verbs for the Football Picture Story

bash, be, break, come, get, go, have, hit, kick, look, make, play, point, run, say, see, shout, smash, smile, stand, tell, throw, walk.

Adjectives

'Technical'

1 They can operate as head-words of nominal groups occurring as Complement in the clause or as modifying-words in nominal groups occurring at this element and at the Subject in the clause.
2 Almost all adjectives may be intensified by a group of submodifiers which includes *very, so, too*, etc.
3 Adjectives enter into a system of comparison whose terms are 'superlative', 'comparative' and 'neutral'. The superlative and comparative terms are realised by *most* and *more* respectively in the case of some adjectives, e.g. *beautiful*, and by *-est* and *-er* in the case of other adjectives, e.g. *long*. Many adjectives, it seems, permit a choice of either *most* or *-est* and of either *more* or *-er*.

'Non-technical'

1 May fill the following blanks:

              Frame A
    The   concert is/was
e.g.   good   good
      bad   bad
Other examples:
    He is a good man.
    He is good.

2 Almost all adjectives may be preceded by *very, quite, so, too*, etc.
    e.g. very beautiful
        quite sweet
3 Some adjectives may be preceded by *more, most*
    e.g. more beautiful
        the most beautiful
4 Other adjectives may end in *-er* and *-est*
    e.g. sweeter
        sweetest

5 Some adjectives end in *-ed*, *-en*, *-ing*
e.g. An exciting play
This play is exciting.
N.B. words with these endings are not adjectives unless they can be preceded by *very*, *quite*, *more*, *most*, etc.

List of adjectives for the Football Picture Story
angry, bad, cross, frightened, naughty, worried.

Adverbs

'Technical'
1 They operate as adjunct in clause structure. They usually occur in final position as in Frames A, B, C and second blank in Frame D, but they can also occur elsewhere; for example, in the initial position (consider the first blank in Frame D).
2 Some adverbs - those that have the morphological structure 'adjective + *-ly* suffix' may intensify adjectives in the modifier of the nominal group, e.g. a temptingly beautiful hat.
3 Many adverbs may be intensified by a group of sub-modifiers which includes *very*, *so*, *too*, etc.
4 Some adverbs enter into a system of comparison which is very similar to that into which adjectives enter, e.g. more beautifully than, most beautifully of all, faster than, fastest of all.
5 The most common functions of the adverb are to locate the process referred to by the verb in terms of time or space (see Frame D).

'Non-technical'
1 May fill one of the following blanks:

Frame A
The little boy is/was frightened
e.g.   now,
                 then

Frame B
The boys ran home
e.g.   quick (-ly, -er),
                 fast (-er)

Frame C
The lady came/went
e.g.   out
                 downstairs
(NOTE: *Not* 'The lady came *out* of the house)

Frame D
are the boys
e.g. There   there
     Here   here
        they ran

                 e.g.   Then   away
                         Soon   off
2 Adverbs most frequently occur in the final position in the clause
(Frames A, B and C), but some can also occur elsewhere in the clause,
for example, in the initial position (Frame D). They can then be seen as
stressed words which function as pointers,
        e.g. *There's* a man,
or as temporal markers,
        e.g. *Soon* they all ran home.
3 Adverbs can occur concurrently. If they belong to the same sub-group
(time, place, manner, etc.) they are usually joined by 'and' or 'but'. e.g.
The ball bounced *up* and *down*; They ran *quickly* but *quietly*. Other-
wise, when one or more adverbs belonging to different sub-groups occur
concurrently, no connecting word occurs.
        e.g. They ran *away then*; He came *out quickly*.

ANALYSIS OF VARIANCE TABLES [*]
TOKEN NOUNS: SUB-SAMPLE 1

Source	d.f.	S.S.	V.E.	F.	Sig. level
Between Class (C)	1	5985.80	5985.80	8.8	$p < .01$
Between Verbal Ability (V.A.)	1	1496.45	1496.45	2.2	N.S.
Between Sex (S)	1	238.20	238.20	-	N.S.
Between Comm. Index (0)	1	7.20	7.2	-	N.S.
1st order inter-actions					
C x V.A.	1	3125.00	3125.0	4.6	$p < .05$
C x S	1	369.65	369.65	-	N.S.
C x O	1	361.25	361.25	-	N.S.
V.A.x S	1	251.90	251.90	-	N.S.
V.A.x O	1	304.20	304.20	-	N.S.
S.x O	1	404.85	404.85	-	N.S.
2nd order inter-actions.					
C x V.A. x S	1	259.35	259.35	-	N.S.
C x S x O	1	378.60	378.60	-	N.S.
C x V.A. x O	1	530.45	530.45	-	N.S.
V.A. x S x O	1	273.95	273.95	-	N.S.
3rd order inter-actions					
C x V.A. x S x O	1	378.30	378.3	-	N.S.
Residual	64	43452.40	679		
TOTAL	79	57817.55			

[*] The analyses presented in these tables are limited to those in which significant differences were revealed.

TOKEN NOUNS: SUB-SAMPLE 2

Source	d.f.	S.S.	V.E.	F.	Sig. level
Between Class (C)	1	4752.60	4752.60	6.9	$p. < 0.25$
Between Verbal Ability (V.A.)	2	802.04	401.02	-	N.S.
Between Sex (S)	1	552.07	552.07	-	N.S.
1st order interactions					
C x V.A.	2	3537.10	1768.55	2.5	N.S.
C x S	1	106.67	106.67	-	N.S.
V.A.x S	2	106.63	53.31	-	N.S.
2nd order interaction					
C x V.A. x S	2	837.43	418.71	-	N.S.
Residual	48	32810.40	683		
TOTAL	59	43504.94			

67

TYPE NOUNS: SUB-SAMPLE 1

Source	d.f.	S.S.	V.E.	F.	Sig.level
Between Class (C)	1	3175.20	3175.20	19.24	$p < .001$
Between Verbal Ability (V.A.	1	605.00	605.00	3.66	N.S.
Between Sex (S)	1	31.25	31.25	-	N.S.
Between Comm. Index (O)	1	14.45	14.45	-	N.S.
1st order interactions					
C x V.A.	1	756.45	756.45	4.58	$p < .05$
C x S	1	156.80	156.80	-	N.S.
C x O	1	145.80	145.80	-	N.S.
V.A. x S	1	7.20	7.20	-	N.S.
V.A. x O	1	12.80	12.80	-	N.S.
S x O	1	224.45	224.45	-	N.S.
2nd order interactions					
C x V.A. x S	1	6.05	6.05	-	N.S.
C x S x O	1	80.00	80.00	-	N.S.
C x V.A. x O	1	92.45	92.45	-	N.S.
V.A. x S x O	1	12.80	12.80	-	N.S.
3rd order interaction					
C x V.A. x S x O	1	162.45	162.45	-	N.S.
Residual	64	10614.80	165		
TOTAL	79	16097.95			

TYPE NOUNS: SUB-SAMPLE 2

Source	d.f.	S.S.	V.E.	F	Sig.level
Between Class (C)	1	2613.60	2613.60	15.3	$p < .001$
Between Verbal Ability (V.A.)	2	537.74	268.42	-	N.S.
Between Sex (S)	1	123.27	123.27	-	N.S.
1st Order interactions					
C x V.A.	2	821.20	410.60	2.4	N.S.
C x S	1	5.40	5.40	-	N.S.
V.A. x S	2	90.53	45.26	-	N.S.
2nd Order interactions					
C x V.A. x S	2	174.40	87.20	-	N.S.
Residual	48	8167.60	170		
TOTAL	59	12533.74			

68

TOKEN VERBS: SUB-SAMPLE 1

Source	d.f.	S.S.	V.E.	F.	Sig.level
Between Class (C)	1	3062.81	3062.81	25.9	p<.001
Between Verbal Ability (V.A.)	1	270.11	270.11	2.2.	N.S.
Between Sex (S)	1	851.51	851.51	7.2	p<.01
Between Comm. Index (O)	1	738.11	738.11	6.2	p<.025
1st order interactions					
C x V.A.	1	4425.32	4425.32	37.5	p<.001
C x S	1	1386.12	1386.12	11.7	p<.01
C x O	1	227.82	227.82	-	N.S.
V.A x S	1	357.02	357.02	3.0	N S.
V.A.x O	1	3062.82	3062.82	25.9	p<.001
S x O	1	678.62	678.62	5.7	p<.025
2nd order interactions					
C x V.A. x S	1	78.00	78.00	-	N.S.
C x S x O	1	46.50	46.50	-	N.S.
C x V.A. x O	1	15.30	15.30	-	N.S.
V.A. x S x O	1	.10	.10	-	N.S.
3rd order interaction					
C x V.A. x S x O	1	.63	.63	-	N.S.
Residual	64	75677.60	118		
TOTAL	79	90878.39			

TOKEN VERBS: SUB-SAMPLE 2

Source	d.f.	S.S.	V.E.	F.	Sig. level
Between Class (C)	1	66.15	66.15	-	N.S.
Between Verbal Ability (V.A.)	2	2399.70	1199.70	1.5	N.S.
Between Sex (S)	1	62.01	62.01	-	N.S.
1st order interactions					
C x (V.A.)	2	3388.30	1694.15	2.1	N.S.
C x S	1	212.82	212.82	-	N.S.
V.A. x S	2	409.04	204.52	-	N.S.
2nd order interaction					
C x V.A. x S	2	308.43	154.21	-	N.S.
Residual	48	37662.40	784		
TOTAL	59	44508.85			

69

TYPE ADJECTIVES: SUB-SAMPLE 1

Source	d.f.	S.S.	V.E.	F.	Sig.level
Between Class (C)	1	148.51	148.51	9.84	p < .01
Between Verbal Ability (V.A.)	1	10.51	10.51	-	N.S.
Between Sex (S)	1	63.01	63.01	4.17	p < .05
Between Comm. Index (O)	1	10.51	10.51	-	N.S.
1st order interactions					
C x V.A.	1	70.32	70.32	4.66	p < .05
C x S	1	6.62	6.62	-	N.S.
C x O	1	23.12	23.12	-	N.S.
V.A. x S	1	15.32	15.32	-	N.S.
V.A. x O	1	2.82	2.82	-	N.S.
S x O	1	13.62	13.62	-	N.S.
2nd order interactions					
C x V.A. x S	1	25.30	25.30	-	N.S.
C x S x O	1	27.60	27.60	-	N.S.
C x V.A. x O	1	13.60	13.60	-	N.S.
V.A. x S x O	1	2.80	2.80	-	N.S.
3rd order interaction					
C x V.A. x S x O	1	1.03	1.03	-	N.S.
Residual	64	965.80	15.09		
TOTAL	79	1400.49			

TYPE ADJECTIVES: SUB-SAMPLE 2

Source	d.f.	S.S.	V.E.	F.	Sig.level
Between Class (C)	1	84.01	84.01	6.4.	p < .025
Between Verbal Ability (V.A.)	2	79.60	39.80	3.0	N.S.
Between Sex (S)	1	79.35	79.35	6.1	p < .025
1st order interactions					
C x V.A.	2	134.54	67.27	5.1	p < .01
C x S	1	8.82	8.82	-	N.S.
V.A. x S	2	5.20	2.60	-	N.S.
2nd order interaction					
C x V.A. x S	2	8.93	4.46	-	N.S.
Residual	48	662.80	13		
TOTAL	59	1063.25			

70

USE OF 'TO BE': SUB-SAMPLE 1

Source	d.f.	S.S.	V.E.	F.	Sig. level
Between Class (C)	1	344.45	344.45	6.2	p<.025
Between Verbal Ability (V.A.)	1	76.05	76.05	-	N.S.
Between Sex (S)	1	312.05	312.05	5.6	p<.025
Between Comm. Index (O)	1	312.05	312.05	5.6	p<.025
1st order interactions					
C x V.A.	1	281.25	281.25	5.1	p<.05
C x S	1	238.05	238.05	4.3	p<.05
C x O	1	0.45	0.45	-	N.S.
V.A. x S	1	174.05	174.05	3.1	N.S.
V.A. x O	1	101.25	101.25	-	N.S.
S x O	1	281.25	281.25	5.1	p<.05
2nd order interactions					
C x V.A. x S	1	6.05	6.05	-	N.S.
C x S x O	1	84.05	84.05	-	N.S.
C x V.A. x O	1	61.25	61.25	-	N.S.
V.A. x S x O	1	198.45	198.45	3.6	N.S.
3rd order interaction					
C x V.A. x S x O	1	8.45	8.45	-	N.S.
Residual	64	3548.80	55		
TOTAL	79	6027.95			

TYPE VERBS: SUB-SAMPLE 1

Source	d.f.	S.S.	V.E.	F.	Sig. level
Between Class (C)	1	1272.01	1272.01	4.7	p<.05
Between Verbal Ability (V.A.)	1	234.61	234.61	-	N.S.
Between Sex (S)	1	201.61	201.61	-	N.S.
Between Comm. Index (O)	1	505.01	505.01	-	N.S.
1st order interactions					
C x V.A.	1	308.12	308.12	-	N.S.
C x S	1	316.02	316.02	-	N.S.
C x O	1	137.82	137.82	-	N.S.
V.A. x S	1	195.32	195.32	-	N.S.
V.A. x O	1	418.62	418.62	-	N.S.
S x O	1	5.52	5.52	-	N.S.
2nd order interactions					
C x V.A. x S	1	10.50	10.50	-	N.S.
C x S x O	1	.60	.60	-	N.S.
C x V.A. x O	1	154.00	154.00	-	N.S.
V.A. x S x O	1	90.30	90.30	-	N.S.
3rd order interaction					
C x V.A. x S x O	1	52.83	52.83	-	N.S.
Residual	64	17042.80	266		
TOTAL	79	20945.69			

TOKEN ADVERBS: SUB-SAMPLE 1

Source	d.f.	S.S.	V.E.	F.	Sig. level
Between Class (C)	1	490.05	490.05	2.4	N.S.
Between Verbal Ability (V.A.)	1	1843.20	1843.20	9.1	p<.01
Between Sex (S)	1	115.20	115.20	-	N.S.
Between Comm. Index (O)	1	405.00	405.00	2.0	N.S.
1st order interactions					
C x V.A.	1	204.80	204.80	-	N.S.
C x S	1	16.20	16.20	-	N.S.
C x O	1	369.80	369.80	-	N.S.
V.A. x S	1	8.45	8.45	-	N.S.
V.A. x O	1	224.45	224.45	-	N.S.
S x O	1	54.45	54.45	-	N.S.
2nd order interactions					
C x V.A. x S	1	266.45	266.45	-	N.S.
C x S x O	1	101.25	101.25	-	N.S.
C x V.A. x O	1	36.45	36.45	-	N.S.
V.A. x S x O	1	51.20	51.20	-	N.S.
3rd order interaction					
C x V.A. x S x O	1	125.00	125.00	-	N.S.
Residual	64	12958.80	202		
TOTAL	79	17270.75			

TYPE ADVERBS: SUB-SAMPLE 1

Source	d.f.	S.S.	V.E.	F.	Sig. level
Between Class (C)	1	7.20	7.20	-	N.S.
Between Verbal Ability (V.A.)	1	204.80	204.80	9.7	p<.01
Between Sex (S)	1	6.05	6.05	-	N.S.
Between Comm. Index (O)	1	18.05	18.05	-	N.S.
1st order interactions					
C x V.A.	1	1.25	1.25	-	N.S.
C x S	1	1.80	1.80	-	N.S.
C x O	1	39.20	39.20	1.8	N.S.
V.A. x S	1	7.20	7.20	-	N.S.
V.A. x O	1	7.20	7.20	-	N.S.
S x O	1	2.45	2.45	-	N.S.
2nd order interactions					
C x V.A. x S	1	8.45	8.45	-	N.S.
C x S x O	1	0.20	0.20	-	N.S.
C x V.A. x O	1	14.45	14.45	-	N.S.
V.A. x S x O	1	3.20	3.20	-	N.S.
3rd order interaction					
C x V.A. x S x O	1	14.45	14.45	-	N.S.
Residual	64	1371.60	21		
TOTAL	79	1707.55			

TOKEN ADVERBS: SUB-SAMPLE 3

Source	d.f.	S.S.	V.E.	F.	Sig. level
Between Verbal Ability (V.A.)	2	3202.54	1601.27	10.3	$p < .001$
Between Sex (S)	1	299.27	299.27	-	N.S.
Between Comm. Index (O)	1	1215.00	1215.00	7.8	$p < .01$
1st order interactions					
V.A. x S	2				
V.A. x O	2	1181.20	590.60	3.8	$p < .05$
S x O	1				
2nd order interaction					
V.A. x S x O	2				
Residual	48	7486.00	155		
TOTAL	59				

TOKEN ADJECTIVES: SUB-SAMPLE 3

Source	d.f.	S.S.	V.E.	F.	Sig.level
Between Verbal Ability (V.A.)	2	20.64	10.32	-	N.S.
Between Sex (S)	1	170.02	170.02	8.9	$p < .01$
Between Comm. Index (O)	1	7.35	7.35	-	N.S.
1st order interactions					
(V.A) x S	2	8.03	4.01	-	N.S.
(V.A.) x O	2	6.02	3.01	-	N.S.
S x O	1				
2nd order interaction					
(V.A.) x S x O	2				
Residual	48	926.00	19		
TOTAL	59				

73

TYPE ADJECTIVES: SUB-SAMPLE 3

Source	d.f.	S.S.	V.E.	F.	Sig.level
Between Verbal Ability (V.A.)	2	17.64	8.37	-	N.S.
Between Sex (S)	1	62.02	62.02	12.44	$p < .01$
Between Comm. Index (O)	1				
1st order interactions					
(V.A.) x S	2				
(V.A.) x O	2				
S x O	1				
2nd order interation					
V.A. x S x O	2				
Residual	48	287.60	5		
TOTAL	59				

ANALYSIS OF VARIANCE: TOTAL TASK SPEECH

Source	d.f.	S.S.	V.E.	F.	Sig. level
Between Class (C)	1	35280.00	35280.00	-	N.S.
Between Verbal Ability (V.A.)	1	15070.05	15070.05	-	N.S.
Between Sex (S)	1	6480.00	6480.00	-	N.S.
Between Comm. (O) Index	1	27528.25	27528.25	-	N.S.
1st order interactions					
C x V.A.	1	25860.50	25860.50	-	N.S.
C x S	1	51714.45	51714.45	2.79	N.S.
C x O	1	21846.00	21846.00	-	N.S.
V.A. x S	1	520.20	520.20	-	N.S.
V.A. x O	1	4748.75	4748.75	-	N.S.
S x O	1	162.40	162.40	-	N.S.
2nd order interactions					
C x V.A. x S	1	5211.55	5211.55	-	N.S.
C x S x O	1	34944.85	34944.85	-	N.S.
C x V.A. x O	1	2652.00	2652.00	-	N.S.
V.A. x S x O	1	24374.10	24374.10	-	N.S.
3rd order interaction					
C x V.A. x S. x O	1	925.25	925.25	-	N.S.
Residual	64	1162206.00	18159		
TOTAL	79	1419524.35			

74

TABLE OF
MEAN FORM-CLASS SCORES WITHIN EACH SUB-SAMPLE *

TOKEN NOUNS

Sub-Sample 1:   M.C.   W.C.

N = 80 $\bar{x}$ 77.07   59.77

                     M.C.   W.C.

          HIGH V.A.   MED. V.A.   HIGH V.A.   MED. V.A.

$\bar{x}$ 87.65   66.50   57.85   61.70

Sub-Sample 2:   M.C.   W.C.

N = 60 $\bar{x}$ 75.49   57.69

TYPE NOUNS

Sub-Sample 1:   M.C.   W.C.

N = 80 $\bar{x}$ 52.07   39.47

                     M.C.   W.C.

          HIGH V.A.   MED. V.A.   HIGH V.A.   MED. V.A.

$\bar{x}$ 57.90   46.25   39.15   44.90

Sub-Sample 2:   M.C.   W.C.

N = 60 $\bar{x}$ 50.86   37.66

TOKEN ADJECTIVES

Sub-Sample 3:   W.C. BOYS   W.C. GIRLS

N = 60 $\bar{x}$ 3.30   6.66

TYPE ADJECTIVES

Sub-Sample 1:   M.C.   W.C.

N = 80 $\bar{x}$ 6.50   3.77

                     BOYS   GIRLS

              $\bar{x}$ 4.25   6.25

                     M.C.   W.C.

          HIGH V.A. MED. V.A.   HIGH V.A.   MED. V.A.

              $\bar{x}$ 7.80   5.20   3.20   4.35

Sub-Sample 2:   M.C.   W.C.

N = 60 $\bar{x}$ 4.45   2.67

                     BOYS   GIRLS

              $\bar{x}$ 2.70   4.45

          HIGH V.A.   MED. V.A.   LOW V.A.   HIGH V.A.   MED. V.A.   LOW V.A.

$\bar{x}$ 9.30   5.50   3.00   2.80   4.40   3.50

Sub-Sample 3:   W.C. BOYS   W.C. GIRLS

N = 60 $\bar{x}$ 2.56   4.60

*The mean form class scores presented in these tables are limited to the mean scores
of those groups which showed significant differences in form class usage.

75

TOKEN VERBS

Sub-Sample 1:		M.C.		W.C.	
N = 80	x̄	87.47		75.10	
		BOYS		GIRLS	
	x̄	84.69		78.02	
		HIGH COMM. INDEX		LOW COMM. INDEX	
	x̄	78.25		84.32	

		M.C.		W.C.	
		HIGH V.A.	MED. V.A.	HIGH V.A.	MED.V.A.
	x̄	96.75	78.20	69.50	80.70

		M.C.		W.C.	
		BOYS	GIRLS	BOYS	GIRLS
	x̄	94.90	80.05	72.20	76.00

		HIGH V.A.		MED. V.A.	
		HIGH COMM.	LOW COMM.	HIGH COMM.	LOW COMM.
	x̄	73.90	92.35	82.60	76.30

		BOYS		GIRLS	
		HIGH COMM.	LOW COMM.	HIGH COMM.	LOW COMM.
	x̄	78.60	90.50	77.90	78.15

USE OF 'TO BE

Sub-Sample 1:		M.C.		W.C.	
N = 80	x̄	15.82		11.65	
		BOYS		GIRLS	
	x̄	15.70		11.75	
		HIGH COMM.		LOW COMM.	
	x̄	11.75		15.7	

		M.C.		W.C.	
		HIGH V.A.	MED.V.A	HIGH V.A.	MED. V.A.
	x̄	18.65	12.95	10.75	12.55

		M.C.		W.C.	
		BOYS	GIRLS	BOYS	GIRLS
	x̄	19.50	12.10	11.90	11.40

		BOYS		GIRLS	
		HIGH COMM.	LOW COMM.	HIGH COMM.	LOW COMM.
	x̄	11.85	19.55	11.65	11.85

TYPE VERBS

Sub-Sample 1:					
N = 80		M.C.		W.C.	
	x̄	54.42		46.45	

TOKEN ADVERBS

Sub-Sample 1:		HIGH V.A.		MED.V.A.	
N = 80	x̄	13.82		25.92	

76

TABLE OF MEAN FORM-CLASS SCORES WITHIN EACH
SUB-SAMPLE (Contd.)

TOKEN ADVERBS (Contd.)

Sub-Sample 3:		HIGH V.A.	MEDIUM V.A.	LOW V.A.
N = 60	x̄	17.20	35.00	27.70

		HIGH COMM.	LOW COMM.
	x̄	31.13	22.13

	HIGH COMM.			LOW COMM.		
	High V.A.	Med.V.A.	Low V.A.	High V.A.	Med.V.A.	Low V.A.
x̄	20.60	45.40	27.40	13.80	24.30	28.00

TYPE ADVERBS

Sub-Sample 1:		HIGH V.A.	MEDIUM V.A.
N = 80	x̄	9.57	10.27

TOTAL TASK SPEECH

Sub-Sample 1:		M.C.	W.C.
	x̄	419.67	377.67
		BOYS	GIRLS
	x̄	407.67	389.67
		HIGH V.A.	MED. V.A.
	x̄	412.40	384.95
		HIGH COMM.	LOW COMM.
N = 80	x̄	417.22	380.12

Sub-Sample 2:		M.C.	W.C.
N = 60	x̄	394.06	391.26
		BOYS	GIRLS
	x̄	390.53	394.80

		HIGH V.A.	MED. V.A.	LOW V.A.
	x̄	422.85	411.10	343.55

Sub-Sample 3:		BOYS	GIRLS
N = 60	x̄	370.73	372.76

		HIGH V.A.	MED. V.A.	LOW V.A.
	x̄	373.40	381.95	359.90

		HIGH COMM.	LOW COMM.
	x̄	391.26	352.23

Mean Scores – Total Task Speech*

	HIGH COMMUNICATION INDEX			LOW COMMUNICATION INDEX		
	High V.A.	Med. V.A.	Low V.A.	High V.A.	Med. V.A.	Low V.A.
Middle Class BOYS	458.4	409.2	296.4	534.4	414.4	
Middle Class GIRLS	434.4	364.8	381.2	378.4	343.4	
Working Class BOYS	373.0	458.6	347.6	330.0	283.4	431.8
Working Class GIRLS	425.6	393.8	349.0	365.0	392.0	311.2

*This table should be examined in conjunction with the analysis of variance table for total task speech, which is concerned with the most critical sub-sample comparisons

Chapter II

SOCIAL CLASS DIFFERENCES IN FORM-CLASS SWITCHING AMONG FIVE-YEAR-OLD CHILDREN
D. Henderson

Introduction

The first part of this analysis revealed a consistent relationship between form-class usage and the social class of the children's parents. Middle class children showed a greater emphasis on lexical differentiation within the nominal group which was manifested by their high scores in the use of nouns and adjectives. This finding is interesting and suggestive, but it will be remembered that the scores for each child were obtained by summing the totals for the three tasks. This raised a number of questions:

1 Did the tasks act selectively on form-class usage? For example, did the children use a significantly greater proportion of their token nouns on the Trotin Cards, and a significantly greater proportion of token verbs on the Picture Stories?

2 Were there task differences in the direction of form-class allocation and were these differences related to any of the major variables? For example, did some children use the highest proportion of adverbs, etc., on the Trotin Cards, whilst others used the highest proportion on the Picture Stories?

3 Was the frequency of significant proportional changes on the form-class measures related to any of the major variables? For example, were there more significant proportional changes among children of one social class, compared to the other social class?

We should stress that this part of the analysis was undertaken for exploratory purposes and very few predictions were made about the possible outcome. The analysis is offered in an attempt to encourage further research into the contextual dependence of linguistic usage.

We hoped that the investigation might reveal differences in the relative sensitivity of the children to the verbal demands of each task, since the tasks were specifically chosen to elicit three distinct types of speech. It was thought possible that the use of some form-classes would prove to be context-dependent whilst others would prove to be used independently of the context. A significant proportional change in the use of a form-class between two tasks, perhaps, suggests that the child is sensitive to the differential verbal demands of each task. For example, we thought that the

79

Trotin Cards would elicit the highest proportion of nouns. This does not necessarily mean that the differential allocation is always *appropriate* to the demands of the task. If a number of significant proportional form-class changes are found between two tasks, it, perhaps, suggests that the child is highly sensitive to the differential verbal demands of the tasks. This is not to say that if no such significant proportional changes are found in a child's speech he or she is insensitive to the *differences* between the tasks. What such a finding may mean is that the child is unable or unwilling to show this sensitivity in his or her linguistic usage.

Before describing the stages of the analysis and the results, two points must be stressed. First, although the figures are not given in this paper, the amount of speech produced by the children when talking about the Elephant was exceedingly small in comparison to the amount of speech produced on the Picture Stories and Trotin Cards. We thought it important to consider proportional changes in form-class usage between comparable amounts of contextual speech, thus the discussion of this analysis will be almost wholly concerned with two of the tasks; the Picture Stories and the Trotin Cards. Secondly, it must be stressed that a significant proportional change in the use of a form-class measure is not necessarily related to the *total* count for that form-class: a child who used a total of 40 token nouns across all the tasks, and distributed them 10, 20, 10, showed the same proportional change as a child who used a total of 80 token nouns across all the tasks and distributed them 20, 40, 20.

The Analysis

Each of the tasks were considered separately. The total raw score on each task for each form-class measure was expressed as a percentage of the child's overall total score on that measure. For example, if a child used a total of 50 type nouns, 15 of which were used on the Picture Stories, 30 of which were used on the Trotin Cards, and 5 of which were used on the Elephant, this was expressed as 30% on the Picture Stories, 60% on the Trotin Cards and 10% on the Elephant. Thus each child in the factorial sample had three percentage scores for each of the following form-class measures:

1 Token nouns
2 Type nouns
3 Token verbs
4 Type verbs
5 Token adverbs
6 Type adverbs
7 Token adjectives
8 Type adjectives

80

Then the median form-class percentages for each task were found. It was then possible to examine the median distribution of each form-class measure across the three tasks. It was considered that a picture of the form-class distributions (for the whole sample) across the three tasks would give some measure of the task-dependence of form-class usage.

TABLE 1

The median percentages of form-class items
on each of the three tasks

Form-class Measure		Picture Stories	Trotin Cards	Elephant
Median %	Token nouns	35%	58%	7%
"	Type nouns	31%	57%	12%
"	Token adjectives	17%	50%	33%*
"	Type adjectives	20%	50%	30%*
"	Token verbs	45%	45%	10%
"	Type verbs	52%	36%	12%
"	Token adverbs	42%	46%	12%
"	Type adverbs	44%	43%	13%

When we examined the median distributions for each form-class measure it was clear that the tasks were acting selectively in form-class usage. It was thought undesirable to set up an *arbitrary* difference in proportions as the criterion for asserting that a significant change had occurred since there are as yet no standard criteria which define form-class switching. We therefore decided to test the significance of proportional changes by using the Kolmogorov-Smirnov 2-Sample Test. This was

TABLE 2

Percentage differences demanded by the Kolmogorov-
Smirnov 2-Sample Test on each form-class measure

Form-Class Measure	Percentage Difference required by K-S 2-Sample Test	Percentage of Sample Children who achieved a Significant Switch
Token nouns	25	56.3
Type nouns	38	26.3
Token adjectives	40	32.7
Type adjectives	21	39.1
Token verbs	9	58.1
Type verbs	36	10.0
Token adverbs	51	10.0
Type adverbs	18	44.5

*These percentages should be treated with caution because of the low incidence of adjectives on this task.

81

considered to be the most suitable test, since it automatically locates the maximum difference between two samples and tests this difference for significance.* Table 2 shows the proportional difference demanded by the Kolmogorov-Smirnov test for each measure.

This means that a child had to show a proportional difference of 25% between two tasks in order for the differential allocation of nouns to be significant. In other words, a child who used 15% of his token nouns on the Picture Stories and 40% of his token nouns on the Trotin Cards achieved a significant proportional change between the tasks, in the direction of the Trotin Cards. This phenomenon will be called form-class switching.

Finally, the data was examined in order to assess the frequency, type, and direction of form-class switching. This stage of the analysis was carried out in four parts.

(1) The overall percentage of sample children who achieved a significant form-class switch in the use of each form-class was found (see Table 2).

(2) The data was then re-examined in terms of the percentage of children in each social class who achieved a significant form-class switch in the use of each form-class.

TABLE 3

*The percentages of children in each social class who
achieved a significant form-class switch*

MIDDLE CLASS		WORKING CLASS	
Form Class Measure	Percentage of Children Switching	Form Class Measure	Percentage of Children Switching
Token nouns	68.0	Token verbs	55.0
Token verbs	62.0	Token nouns	53.3
Type adverbs	52.0	Type adverbs	38.8
Type adjectives	40.0	Type adjectives	38.3
Token adjectives	34.0	Token adjectives	31.6
Type nouns	30.0	Type nouns	23.3
Type verbs	12.0	Type verbs	8.3
Token adverbs	12.0	Token adverbs	8.3

(3) The percentage of children in each social class who achieved *frequent* form-class switching was found.

*For a full description of this Test, see Siegel, S. (1956) *Non-Parametric Statistics for the Behavioral Sciences*, McGraw Hill, pp. 127–136.

82

TABLE 4

Frequency of form-class switching between each social class

	MIDDLE CLASS (N = 50)		WORKING CLASS (N = 60)	
Number of Form-Class Switches	% Sample Switching	N	% Sample Switching	N
1	10.0	5	25.0	15
2	28.0	14	31.6	19
3	32.0	16	11.6	9
4	6.0	3	5.0	3

Within each social class the data was further examined in terms of sex, verbal ability scores and Communication Index ratings.

TABLE 5

Frequent* form-class switching within each social class

		SEX		VERBAL ABILITY			COMMUNICATION INDEX	
		Boys	Girls	High V.A.	Med. V.A.	Low V.A.	High Comm.	Low Comm.
MIDDLE CLASS	N	25	25	20	20	10	30	20
% Children who achieved frequent switching		44.0	32.0	40.0	30.0	50.0	33.3	45.0
	N =	11	8	8	6	5	10	9
		Boys	Girls	High V.A.	Med V.A.	Low V.A.	High Comm.	Low Comm.
WORKING CLASS	N	30	30	20	20	20	30	30
% Children who achieved frequent switching		20	20.0	20.0	20.0	20.0	13.3	26.6
	N =	6	6	4	4	4	4	8

* Significant switches on at least three or four form-class measures (token nouns, type nouns, token verbs, type adverbs) is defined as frequent form-class switching.

Significant form-class switching on at least three of four possible measures was defined as *frequent* form-class switching. The four measures were token nouns, type nouns, token verbs and type adverbs. (The criteria for isolating these four measures will be explained in the examination of the results of this analysis.)

(4) The direction of significant form-class switching in the use of token nouns, type nouns, token verbs and type adverbs was determined.

TABLE 6

The direction of significant form-class switches on
four form-class measures

		% Children who Switched to Trotin		% Children who Switched to Picture Stories	
		Middle Class	Working Class	Middle Class	Working Class
TOKEN NOUNS		100.0	87.5	-	9.3
	N =	30	28	0	3
TYPE NOUNS		93.0	85.7	-	-
	N =	14	12	0	0
TOKEN VERBS		44.4	37.9	55.5	62.0
	N =	12	11	15	18
TYPE ADVERBS		36.3	17.6	40.9	35.2
	N =	8	3	9	6

NOTE: Children who switched between the Picture Stories and the
Elephant or between the Trotin Cards and the Elephant are
excluded from this analysis.

The direction of switching among middle class children was then compared with the direction of switching among working class children. In this way, some knowledge was gained of the relative context-dependence of each of these measures for the children in each social class.

The Results of the Analysis

The Median Form-Class Percentage for each Task
Table 1 shows the median proportional allocation for each form-class measure across the three tasks. However, it should be remembered that the amount of speech produced when the children were talking about the Elephant was much smaller than the amounts produced when they were talking about the Picture Stories or the Trotin Cards, therefore the median percentages shown on the Elephant should be treated with caution. It is clear from Table 1 that the tasks acted selectively in the production of all the form-class measures, but if the Elephant is excluded from the comparison it will be seen that the Trotin Cards acted selectively in the use of token and type nouns and token and type adjectives, but that the Picture Stories acted selectively in the use of type verbs. The children as a whole made little or no distinction between the Picture Stories and the Trotin Cards in the use of token verbs and token and type adverbs. The percentage scores shown on the Elephant in the use of adjectives may appear suggestive, but two qualifications must be pointed out. Fifty-nine of the children in the sample did not use adjectives at all when talking about the Elephant and therefore the median percentages are based upon a sample of only 51 children. Perhaps a more important qualification is that the

children as a whole used relatively few adjectives in their total speech. When relatively small numbers are expressed as percentages, the results tend to be misleading.

Results of the Kolmogorov-Smirnov 2-Sample Test

The Kolmogorov-Smirnov 2-Sample Test showed the proportional difference in percentages needed between two tasks in order that the difference could be said to be significant (see Table 2). It can be inferred that if proportional differences between two tasks are relatively large in the overall sample, then the percentage difference between the two tasks demanded by the Kolmogorov-Smirnov test in order for the change to be significant will tend to be quite large. On the other hand, if the proportional differences between two tasks are relatively small in the overall sample, the percentage difference between the two tasks demanded by the Kolmogorov-Smirnov test in order for the change to be significant will tend to be much smaller.* Bearing this inference in mind, Table 2 suggests that there were very small overall differences in the proportional allocation of token verbs across the tasks, but very large overall differences in the proportional allocation of token adverbs and token adjectives across the three tasks. This finding is illuminated in the case of token adjectives by Table 1, which shows the median proportional allocations. In the case of token adverbs, the picture is not so clear, since the median percentage of token adverbs used on the Picture Stories is almost the same as the median percentage of token adverbs used on the Trotin Cards. The only implication that can be drawn from the results is that the variance between individual children must be very large in the allocation of token adverbs.

Criteria for the Selection of Form-Classes

It was decided to omit four of the form-class measures from further examination of the data. The measures omitted were token and type adjectives, type verbs and token adverbs. Token and type adjectives were omitted because of the scarcity of these form-class items, and the consequent danger of misleading results. For example, a child who used 1 adjective on the Picture Stories, 3 on the Trotin Cards and 2 on the Elephant would show percentage scores of 16.6%, 50%, and 33.4%. This would undoubtedly be defined as significant form-class switching, but given such a small number of items such a distribution would well have arisen by chance. Type verbs and token adverbs were omitted because of the small number of children in the sample who achieved significant form-class switching on these measures — only 10% of the sample switched on

---

*For example, if the mean percentage difference between two tasks for the whole sample is 25.0%, then the Kolmogorov-Smirnov 2-Sample Test will demand a proportional difference significantly in excess of 25.0%. However, if the mean percentage difference between two tasks for the whole sample is only 9.0%, then the proportional difference demanded by the Kolmogorov-Smirnov 2-Sample Test will be much lower.

each of these measures. Only token nouns, type nouns, token verbs and type adverbs satisfied the two conditions for a useful analysis of the data: a high percentage of children changing the proportional allocation of a particular form-class and frequent use of the form-class.

Form-Class Switching and Social Class
Table 3 shows the percentage of children in each social class who achieved a significant form-class switch between two tasks for the eight form-class measures. This table has been arranged in order to show that the variation in the percentage of children who switch their form-class use follows an almost identical pattern in *each* social class. However, more middle class children achieved form-class switching than working class children on *all* the measures. The differences are most marked in the case of token and type nouns, token verbs and type adverbs. Nearly 15% more middle class children than working class children showed significant form-class switching on token nouns. About 7% more middle class children showed significant form-class switching on type nouns and token verbs. Approximately 13% more middle class children showed significant form-class switching on type adverbs.

Social Class Differences in the Frequency of Form-Class Switching.
The frequency of form-class switching was examined for token nouns, type nouns, token verbs and type adverbs. It will be remembered that the criteria which determined selection were that the number of children involved should be reasonably large and the number of form-class items should also be reasonably large. It was possible for a child to show a form-class switch on any or all of these measures. This meant that a child could have a score of one, two, three or four switches. Children who switched on three or four of these measures were defined as frequent switchers. The results are shown in Table 4. Thirty-eight per cent of the middle class children in the sample showed frequent switching compared to only 20% of the working class children in the sample. Whilst 10% of the middle class children switched on only one of the measures, 25% of the working class children switched on only one measure.

TABLE 7
NUMBER OF CHILDREN SWITCHING

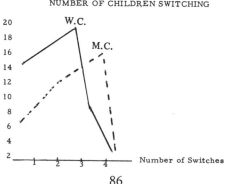

86

The graph shows very clearly that middle class children tended to switch more frequently than working class children. When working class children did switch, they tended to switch on fewer measures.

The frequency of switching is not related to the sex, verbal ability scores or Communication Index ratings of the children. However, there was a very slight tendency for frequent switching among middle class children to be related to their verbal ability scores (see Table 5). Since the numbers involved are very small, this finding should be treated with extreme caution.

The Task-Dependence of Form-Class Usage
The task-dependence of form-class usage was assessed by examining the direction of significant switching on each of the four form-classes. Although no figure is given in the paper, we considered that the amount of speech produced by the children when talking about the Elephant was too small for this task to be compared with the other two tasks. We decided to limit this part of the investigation to differences in the direction of switching between the Picture Stories and the Trotin Cards. The direction of significant switching on each form-class was examined for each social class (see Table 6). A very clear pattern is revealed in the case of token nouns and type nouns. The great majority of the children who achieved significant switching on token and type nouns allocated these form-classes to the Trotin Cards. All children, irrespective of social class, behaved in this way.

A rather different pattern emerged in the case of token verbs and type adverbs. Working class children tended to allocate the highest proportion of their token verbs and of their type adverbs to the Picture Stories. No such consistency emerged among middle class children. Middle class children on the other hand are just as likely to allocate the highest proportion of their token verbs and their type adverbs to either the Picture Stories or the Trotin Cards.

Discussion
The first stage of this analysis of form-class usage revealed a greater emphasis on lexical differentiation within the nominal group on the part of middle class children, and a strong tendency on the part of working class children to use adverbs frequently. These findings raised the question of the possible task dependence of the form-class measures. Were high scores on a form-class measure elicited by a particular task or tasks and were there social class differences in form-class response to a particular task or tasks? We were also interested in the *frequency* of form-class switching among middle class children compared with working class children: in other words, were middle class children more likely to show a greater number of form-class switches than working class children? The direction of frequent form-class switching may not necessarily be

appropriate to the verbal demands of a task as defined by *adult* criteria, as five-year-old children may be operating with rather different criteria. We tentatively thought that the relative frequency of form-class switching might indicate differences in one measure of linguistic flexibility. Degrees of flexibility could be related to forms of socialisation which sensitise the child to the verbal realisation of differences and dissimilarity. This sensitivity to difference could be partly manifested by differences in linguistic usage between contexts. Frequent form-class switching could thus be one indication of verbally realised sensitivity to difference and dissimilarity.

We will now attempt to answer the questions which we have raised in the light of the results of this analysis.

1 Did the tasks act selectively on form-class usage? This question can only be partially answered since the data imposed a number of limitations on the analysis. Because of the very small amount of speech produced by the children when talking about the Elephant, form-class usage on this task could not be compared with the form-class usage on the Picture Stories and the Trotin Cards. It was only possible to make a comparison between two of the tasks. Further limitations were imposed on the analysis. Two of the form-class measures (token adjectives and type adjectives) had to be omitted from the analysis because of the scarcity of form-class items produced by the children on these measures, and two more form-class measures (type verbs and token adverbs) had to be omitted because of the small number of children who achieved significant form-class switching on these measures. The analysis was only able to examine the relative contextual dependence of four measures: token nouns, type nouns, token verbs and type adverbs. Nevertheless, the results show that the use of different nouns (the types) and the frequency with which nouns were used (the tokens) was dependent upon a specific task – the Trotin Cards. This finding supports the prediction which was made in the introduction to this chapter. The majority of children who achieved significant switching on these linguistic form-classes used the highest proportion when talking about the Trotin Cards, irrespective of social class, sex, verbal ability scores or Maternal Communication Index ratings. In the case of token verbs and type adverbs the *overall* sample distribution shows that the use of these two form-classes appears to be independent of the tasks. In fact, the sample distribution of token verbs and type adverbs across the tasks is rather misleading since we found the *direction* of switching on these measures to be related to the social class of the children. We will discuss this finding at greater length when we attempt to answer the second question.

2 Were there social class differences in form-class response to a particular task or tasks?

Again it must be emphasised that this analysis was limited to switching between only two tasks – the Picture Stories and the Trotin

88

Cards – on only four form-class measures. Despite the apparent context-independence of token verbs and type adverbs in the sample as a whole, social class differences in context-dependence were found on these measures. Working class children showed a tendency to use most of their token verbs and type adverbs when talking about the Picture Stories, whereas middle class children as a whole showed no particular task preference in their use of these two form-classes. This raised the question of whether the middle class children had a more open set than working class children in their use of token verbs and type adverbs. It may simply be that there was greater variation among middle class children in the task-dependence of these form-classes. It is hoped that a content analysis, with particular reference to context, will provide an answer to this question.

3 Did the frequency of form-class switching relate to the social class of the children, their sex their verbal ability scores or the Communication Index ratings of their mothers?

The analysis showed that frequent form-class switching was more strongly related to social class than to the other variables. We found that middle class children were more likely to show frequent form-class switching than working class children. Thirty-eight percent of the middle class children switched frequently, whereas only 20% of the working class children switched frequently. On the whole, frequent switching did not appear to be related to the sex, verbal ability scores or Communication Index ratings of the children in either social class. Because no differences were found this does not mean to say that these factors do not influence form-class switching. A large sample is required both of children and contexts before this question can be answered. Nevertheless, our findings in the first stage of this analysis showed that the sex of the children and the Communication Index ratings of their mothers relate to the children's form-class usage.

Whilst the limitations of this analysis should be borne in mind, our findings suggest that the middle class children in our sample show greater linguistic flexibility in their form-class usage than do working class children. We therefore suggest that this finding bears some relation to Bernstein's (1964) hypothesis that the verbal realisation of difference and dissimilarity, which plays an important part in the socialisation of a middle class child, will be reflected in the speech of middle class children. The middle class children in our sample showed a greater frequency of form-class switching between two somewhat dissimilar tasks, which suggests that they were perhaps better able to express verbally their sensitivity to the dissimilarity than working class children. It should again be stressed that this finding does not necessarily mean that the working class children were insensitive to the dissimilarity between the two contexts, but that they were perhaps less able to express their sensitivity through differential allocation of a number of form-class measures.*

The results of this exploratory analysis should be treated with caution, but the analysis may be useful in directing attention to some of the difficulties inherent in the examination of context-dependent speech across a range of contexts. We found that this type of analysis was limited by the small sample of children involved, by the insufficiency of a range of contextual speech samples of comparable size, and by the scarcity of some form-class items in the children's speech. In future research of this kind, it will be necessary to obtain speech from a large sample of carefully matched subjects so that cross-breaks do not unduly reduce the numbers. We think it will also be necessary to offer a wide range of different contexts. This would involve intensive piloting of the contexts in order to ensure that different socio-economic groups, both sexes and all ability ranges were provided with a range of contexts most appropriate to them. The cost of such research would undoubtedly tend to be high, but we feel that the results obtained would justify the expenditure of money and effort. Not only would it then be possible to examine linguistic flexibility across a range of contexts, but intensive piloting might reveal differences in contextual response which would reflect differences in areas of relevance between children in different socio-economic groups, between children of different sex, and between children of different ability.

In this analysis we have drawn attention to the selective function of contexts upon form-class usage. However, we should like to raise the more general question of the selective function of contexts upon grammatical and lexical choices.† If we call the system of context-dependent grammatical and lexical choices a speech variant then we can pursue the question of the range of speech variants available to different children. We can then inquire into the sociological antecedents which affect the range of speech variants. If it is the case that high level controls regulate linguistic usage (Bernstein, 1968) then we can further consider the relationships between such linguistic codes and the range of speech variants which such codes may control. The study of language acquisition implies something more than a study of the child's mastery of the linguistic rule system; it must also examine the social factors which affect the range of contexts which are available for linguistic realisation, and the nature of such realisation. It would then become possible to examine the inter-relationships between the child's exploration of the linguistic rule

*It may be the case that the middle-class children in the sample were better able to obey the interviewer's instructions than the working-class children. The interviewer's opening statements acted as definitions of the contexts. In the case of the Picture Stories, the interviewer told the child that she was going to show some pictures which told a story, and she asked the child to tell the story. In the case of the Trotin Cards, the interviewer asked the child to look at the picture and tell her what was going on in the picture. It is possible that the middle-class children were more likely to decode the interviewer's instructions accurately, and thus differentiate between these two tasks.

†Ervin-Tripp (1964), Grimshaw (1967), Hymes (1962).

system and the social factors which influence the range of relevant contexts and their linguistic realisation.

Conclusions

This analysis was undertaken on the exploratory basis in order to examine (a) possible differences in the context-dependence of various form-class measures and (b) social class differences in the frequency of form-class switching. It must be stressed that this analysis was concerned with a rather small sample of children and differences were examined between only two tasks. Our results should therefore be treated with some caution.

The major finding shows the relationship between social class and frequency of form-class switching. Middle class children tend to switch form-class usage more frequently than working class children. This phenomenon is interpreted as a measure of linguistic flexibility.

The results suggest that there is greater homogeneity in the context-dependence of token verbs and type adverbs among working class children. Working class children tend to allocate the highest proportions of token verbs and type adverbs to the Picture Stories. No overall tendency was observed among middle class children.

We consider that this exploratory analysis has been useful in pointing the way to further research into the inter-relationships between the child's exploration of the linguistic rule system and the social factors which influence the range of contexts which are available for linguistic realisation and the nature of such realisation.

REFERENCES

Bernstein, B. B. (1968) A Socio-Linguistic Approach to Socialisation with some reference to educability. In Gumperz, J. and Hymes, D. H. (Eds.) *Directions in Socio-Linguistics*, New York: Holt, Rinehart and Winston (In press).

Ervin-Tripp, S. (1964e) An Analysis of the Interaction of Language, Topic, and Listener: in Gumperz, J. J. and Hymes, D. H. (Eds.), *The Ethnography of Communication*, special publication of *American Anthropologist*, 66, part 2, No.6

Grimshaw, A. D. (1967) Socio-linguistics. In Wilbert Schramm, Ithiel Pool, Nathan Maccob, Edwin Parker, Frederick Frey and Leonard Fein (Eds.), *Handbook of Communication*, Rand McNally & Co. (In press).

Hymes, D. H. (1962) The Ethnography of Speaking. In Gladwin and Sturtevand, W. C. (Eds.), *Anthropology and Human behaviour*. Washington, D.C.: Anthropology Society of Washington.

Chapter III

SOCIAL CLASS DIFFERENCES IN COMMUNICATION
AND CONTROL
B. Bernstein and W. Brandis

Introduction

In the previous section Dorothy Henderson's research indicated certain relationships between a Communication Index score of mothers' and children's form-class usage. At the time of the analysis of the children's speech we were able only to take advantage of two schedules amongst a number which were concerned with aspects of the mother's communications to her child. In this section we shall report the results obtained when we added to this initial Communication Index other sections of the first maternal interview questionnaire which have a bearing upon processes of communication and control. We shall show in this chapter the associations between this more developed Index of Communication and Control and parental social class, family size, ordinal position of the child, sex of the child, ability and W.I.S.C. scores of the child *and* the associations between the Index and the nature of the boundary the mothers drew between themselves and the school, the potential disagreements between the mothers and the school and the teachers' estimates of the children's future school career. It will not be possible in this chapter to enter into a discussion of the theory from which our research orientation was derived. The theoretical basis of the research will be set out in a future Sociological Research Unit monograph.

The Construction of the Maternal Index of Communication and Control

We should point out that in the first maternal questionnaire, the sections bearing upon the mother's communications were very much concerned with the possible relations of the mother's and child's speech and their relation to the child's cognitive development. We should also emphasise that only a small number of the 48 questions which made up the first maternal interview bore directly upon the area of maternal-child communication. The rest of the questionnaire was more concerned with various aspects of the preparation of the child for his future infant school experience. In the first questionnaire, we were essentially exploring the

93

area of communication with a view to developing it more extensively in the second maternal interview which was to take place in two years time. The Index of Communication and Control was built upon three closed schedules, where the mother ticked or ranked statements and one open schedule, where the mother freely answered pre-determined questions. The components of this Index are the following:

(1) The 'verbal interaction' and 'avoidance' schedules referred to in D. Henderson's research report as the 'Communication Index.'
(2) Aspects of the mothers' reports on how they controlled their children.
(3) Mothers' reported emphasis upon the general explorative/cognitive use of toys.

We shall consider in some detail these components of the Index. The 'avoidance' and the 'verbal interaction' schedules have been described in the previous section. The Appendix II by W. Brandis gives a detailed account of the scoring procedures used, their reliability and rationale.

The Maternal Control Component of the Index

Towards the end of the first maternal interview the mothers were asked how they would deal with their child in six hypothetical situations.* In three of these situations, whatever the mother said she would do, the interviewer then asked what she would next do if the child refused to co-operate. The point of these additional questions was to explore the range of alternatives available to the mothers, if the child initially did not respond appropriately. We constructed a very elaborate coding frame† in order to analyse what the mother said. Sections of this frame were concerned with the rationale the mother offered for what she did or did not do; another section, 'control', dealt with a variety of strategies which did not involve giving reasons to the child; a very elaborate section was concerned with the type and complexity of the reasons offered and whether the consequences of the child's behaviour was referred to the child, to the parent or to someone else. Another section was concerned with the

*These are given in the Appendix by W. Brandis.

†The social control coding frame was constructed by Basil Bernstein and Jenny Cook. An application of this frame will be reported in a future monograph entitled 'Maternal and Child Processes of Communication and Control'. The full account will be reported in Miss Cook's doctoral dissertation. A brief account of the theory underlying our analysis of communication and control is given in Bernstein (1964) 'Family Role Systems, Communication and Socialisation', paper given to the Conference on Research into Childhood and Adolescence, University of Chicago. A more comprehensive account is in Bernstein (1968) 'A Socio-Linguistic Approach to Socialisation' in Directions in Socio-Linguistics (eds) Gumperz, J. and Hymes, D. Holt, Rinehart and Winston (in press).

allocation of blame; there was a section dealing with the type of involvement of the mother in the problem. Finally, there was a section concerned with reparative acts initiated by the mother/parents or child or some combination of both. It was not thought for one moment that all the numerous categories and their sub-divisions would be filled. What we wanted to design was a fairly exhaustive procedure for the analysis of control which had built into it the possibility of testing a particular theory of control. This stresses the nature of its linguistic basis and its consequences for social role learning. The mean number of statements allocated to the various categories of the frame for any one mother is 14 in the working-class area and 15 in the middle-class area. On *a priori*, theoretical grounds we picked out aspects of the *control* section of the frame and aspects of the *appeals* section, (the part dealing with any attempt by the mother to offer an explanation to the child for the required change in his behaviour) which we thought might have the strongest relation to the child's future cognitive development and to his response to control by adults outside of his family.

The *control* section of the frame had categories which dealt with diverting the child, bargaining and offering concessions, anticipating the expected misbehaviour, and arranging the environment so that no confrontation arose. It also had a series of categories for the coding of physical punishment, e.g. 'I'd smack him'; verbal punishment, 'I'd tell him off'; categoric statements, 'I'd make him'. We also tried to cope with social class equivalents in categoric statements, so that the rather more middle-class statement, 'I'd tell him not to make a fuss' was coded under the same category as 'I'd tell him to shut up'. *We used for the construction of the Index, the scores in the 'physical punishment', 'verbal punishment' and 'categoric/imperative' categories.*

The *appeals* section of the frame dealt with the reasons the mother offered *to the child*, in order to change his behaviour. We made a basic distinction between positional appeals and personal appeals to the child. Positional appeals refer the child's behaviour to a rule governing a particular status or social category or class of behaviour, e.g., 'Little boys don't play with dolls', 'Children of your age should be able to......'. 'It's wrong to steal'. Personal appeals are those in which the consequences of the child's behaviour are explained to him, e.g. 'That made mummy very angry', 'If you stay up, you'll be tired in the morning'. Personal appeals in turn are divided into three, in terms of (a) whether the effect or consequence to the parent is emphasised to the child (parent-orientated), (b) where the effect on or consequences for the child is specified (child-orientated) and (c) where the effect on, or consequence for, some other person is specified (other-orientated). Thus personal appeals are distinguished in terms of their referents. Each type of personal appeal is further sub-divided according to whether it is an affective appeal, cognitive, affective/cognitive, or authority reinforcing. In the case of child-orientated appeals there is one more sub-division, 'intent'. This sub-division refers to any statement in which the mother explicitly recognises the positive aspects of the intentions of the child e.g., ' "Darling you meant well", I'd say "That was nice of you to do that but. . . ."' Each statement within the child-orientated division of the general category Personal Appeals was classified according to whether it was simple (only one reason given) or complex (more than one reason given).

We extracted from the *personal* appeals section of the frame all statements which were classified as child-orientated and were allocated to the following categories:

1 Child-orientated cognitive (simple): 'If you don't go to school, you won't learn to read'.
2 Child-orientated cognitive (complex): 'If you stay up you'll be tired in the morning and you won't work well at school'.
3 Child-orientated cognitive/affective: 'If you don't go to school, you won't have any friends and you won't learn *anything*'.
4 Child-orientated — intent: 'I'd say, "I know you meant well but. . . . . ."'

We did not use those statements under the child-orientated classification which were allocated to the affective category e.g. 'You'll feel very miserable/upset/delighted/happy/pleased — if you go on/stop doing that.' Thus we used for the Index, child-orientated appeals which stressed the objective consequences of the child's behaviour for *him* as well as statements which stressed the mother's recognition of the child's intent.

Thus the second component of the Index utilised those aspects of maternal control which consisted of coercive/threatening/imperative statements and those statements which were their antithesis, those which offered the child an explanation of the consequences of his action as they referred to him together with statements which made verbally explicit the mother's recognition of the child's intent in acting as he did.

The Mother's Orientation towards the Uses of Toys*

During the first interview the mother was presented with a list of six limited uses of toys and she was asked to rank them in order of importance†. Although this schedule does not bear directly upon mother-child communication it was included in the Index because of the cognitive

*The argument which follows involves a repetition of the reasoning presented by Brandis in Appendix II.

†A To keep children amused by themselves.
B So that they can play with other children.
C So that they can find out about things.
D To free the mother so that she can do other things.
E To help them when they go to school.
F To show that mother cares when she has been away.

significance of the statement 'C' 'to find out about things'. Of equal significance we believed that a mother who ranked this statement high would also place a high value upon making active, linguistically, the potentialities of toys for her child. On the other hand mothers who ranked 'D' 'To free the mother so that she could do other things', rather high in their preference would be less concerned to mediate the potentialities of toys to her child and more concerned to limit her interactions with her child. When we worked out the average rank for each statement for the total sample of mothers we found that the statement 'C' was clearly differentiated from the other five (average rank 2.06), statements 'E', 'A' and 'B' formed a second set all receiving very similar rankings (3.07, 3.23, 3.37) and statements 'F' and 'D' grouped together (4.40, 4.87). It seemed that we were not entitled to consider statement 'D' 'To free the mother so that she could do other things' as independent of statement 'F' 'To show that mother cares when she's been away'. We therefore decided to put statement 'C' against statements 'D' and 'F'; that is, we would compare mothers in terms of the extent to which 'C' received a high ranking choice and statements 'F' and 'D' received very low ranking choices e.g. fifth or sixth. The reason we offer for such a grouping is that statement 'C' stands apart for it especially refers to the general cognitive/explorative dimension with the possibility of verbal mediation, whereas 'F' and 'D' refer to the uses of toys from the point of view of the *mother* not the child. On the other hand, statements, A, B, E although referring to the child imply less verbal mediation and where they do, as in the case of 'E' it is of a more limited kind. Thus a mother who is high on this component of the Index is a mother who ranks very high 'C' and ranks 'F' and 'D' as fifth or sixth choice. Some justification for this procedure is given by the fact that the correlation between such ranking and a low avoidance score (a mother who reports that she would not avoid or evade answering difficult questions put to her by the child) is 0.37.

We have now given an outline of the components of the Maternal Index of Communication and Control. Thus a low score on this Index is obtained by a mother who reports that:-

1 She is less likely to take up across a range of contexts the child's attempts to talk to her.

2 She is more likely to avoid or evade difficult questions put to her by her child.

3 She is likely to use frequently coercive, threatening or imperative forms of control.

4 She is less likely to use frequently, when controlling her child, explanations of the consequences of the child's acts for *him*.

5 She does not value highly the general explorative/cognitive function of toys and she does *not* reject uses of toys which refer to *her* rather than referring to her child.

97

The five components of the Index, are all intercorrelated, (see Appendix II) and each variable correlates in turn with a range of external variables. But the correlations obtained with the Index, as a whole, are higher with external variables than are the correlations between only one component of the Index and external variables (see Table on p. 144).

The Application of the Index of Communication and Control

We will now set out the relationships between the score on the Index and the following:-
1 Social Class.
2 Ability and W.I.S.C. scores of the children.
3 Family size, ordinal position and sex of the child.
4 The nature of the boundary the mother draws between the home and the school.
5 Disagreements between the home and the school.
6 Teachers' estimates of the child's future school career.

In order to show the differential effects of the Index score the results will be given separately for the middle-class area and the working-class area. We are forced to distinguish areas because of our sampling frame and the distinction suits our purpose insofar as it results in two distinct social class groups. The correlation between area and social class is 0.742.

Social Class and Index Score

In the working class area the correlation between the Index score and social class is 0.41 whilst in the middle-class the correlation between the Index and social class is 0.36. The lower correlation in the middle-class area reflects a greater homogeneity in mother's Index scores. *The correlation between the Index score and social class for the whole sample is 0.57.* (See Appendix III).

Ability Tests

After the children had been in school for three weeks they were given three ability tests, the English Version of the Peabody Picture Vocabulary Test, the Crichton Vocabulary Scale and the Raven's Progressive Matrices. We shall present first the correlations between social classes and the three ability tests for the whole sample, and the correlations between each area and the ability tests. This is followed by the correlations between the Index of Communication and Control and the ability tests for the whole sample and the correlation between the Index score in each area and the ability scores of the children.

Ability Tests
Correlations with Social Class

	W.C. Area (174)	M.C. Area (141)	Total Sample (337)
Matrices	.179	.109	.282
Crichton	.163	.295	.314
EPVT	.137	.341	.383

Correlations with the Maternal Index Score

	W.C. Area (174)	M.C. Area (141)	Total Sample (337)
Matrices	.192	.054	.233
Crichton	.231	.110	.283
EPVT	.251	.225	.347

These results show that as far as the total sample is concerned there is very little to choose between the correlations obtained with social class and those obtained with the Index. In other words we could substitute the Index for social class. However, when we examine the area correlation with the ability scores it is clear that the Index bears a relation with the ability scores only in the working-class area. The index is not sufficiently sensitive to discriminate between mothers in the middle-class area. This result was expected and, in fact, is stated explicitly in a paper written in 1965.

W.I.S.C.

When the children were 6+ they were given the W.I.S.C. Although all children in the working-class area were given the full-scale W.I.S.C. not all the mothers in the area received the first questionnaire. The mothers of the children in the experimental design who were in the three schools designated as Control 2 (see Introduction) were not interviewed as we did not want in any way to influence these mothers in this control group, because of the possible effect on the evaluation of the exploratory language programme. We can therefore only correlate the W.I.S.C. scores in the working-class area with the mothers who were interviewed. As a result the sample size drops from 214 to 162. In the middle-class the shortened form of the W.I.S.C. was given to the total middle-class sample. However we have as yet not transformed these scores into I.Q.'s. *Thus the findings we shall present relate only to the working-class area.*

At the age of five the Index correlations with the three ability tests are higher than the social class correlations. The relative superiority of the Index over social class holds also for the W.I.S.C. scores. The correlation between social class and the W.I.S.C. is 0.25 whereas the correlation between the Index and the W.I.S.C. is 0.38. The Index has a more powerful association with the W.I.S.C. than has social class.

When the children were aged five years, the correlations may have been low because of the general unreliability of the tests, and particularly because of the children's response to the test situation. We should expect the correlations to be higher at 6+ years because the W.I.S.C. is a much more reliable test than the three given to the children when they were five and because the test situation was probably not as disturbing to the children.

So far, we have shown the social class and Index correlations with the ability tests when the children were 5 years of age and the correlation between each of these two variables and the W.I.S.C. scores in the working-class area. We will now examine the relationship between the Index score and family size and the ordinal position of the child. If the Index score of the mother is related to family size and/or ordinal position of the child, then the score on the Index cannot be regarded as representing a sub-cultural phenomenon. If such a relation exists then we would have to conclude that the processes of communication and control as we measured them were simple functions of the size of a family and a child's age position within the family. We shall first look at the relationship between social class and family size. In the working-class area there is a small correlation 0.19 (significant at the 0.05 level) between social class and family size. In the working-class area if the social class of the parents is relatively high then there is a weak tendency for the family size to be small. In the middle-class area there is no relationship between social class position of the parents and the size of the family, presumably because there is much less variation in the size of family in the middle-class area. Despite the small correlation between family size and parental social class in the working-class area there is no significant correlation between size of family and the scores on the Index. In the middle-class area we again find, as we would expect, no correlations between family size and the score on the Index. Let us look now at the relationship between the child's position within the family and the score on the Index. In neither the middle-class area nor the working-class area is there a significant correlation between the ordinal position of the child and the Maternal Index score. Thus in our sample the processes of Maternal Communication and Control are independent of the size of the family and the child's position within the family.

Now let us consider the relationships between family size and ordinal position, to the ability tests and the W.I.S.C. scores. Only in the *working-class* area is there a correlation between family size and the ability and W.I.S.C. scores. In this area and only in this area, there is a weak tendency ($r = 0.16$ significant at 0.05 level) for the children in smaller families to have Higher ability and W.I.S.C. scores. If we now look at the relationship between ordinal position and ability and W.I.S.C. scores (partialling out family size) we find one rather surprising result. There is no relationship in either area between the ordinal position of the child and his score on the

Crichton, Matrices or W.I.S.C. However, in *both* the middle-class and working-class there is a small but significant correlation between the younger children and a high score on the E.P.V.T. In the working-class area, when we control for family size, we find a correlation of 0.21 (significant at the 0.01 level) between younger children and high E.P.V.T. scores, and in the middle-class area, when we control for family size, we find again a correlation, between younger children and high scores on the E.P.V.T. (r = 0.17 significant at the 0.05 level).

The effect of controlling for family size in these comparisons is virtually to restrict the comparison between ordinal position of the children and high E.P.V.T. scores to the relatively larger families. It is worth-while drawing attention to the fact that when we control for family size in both areas, parental social class is not significantly related to the E.P.V.T. scores in the working-class area but High Maternal scores on the Index is correlated with high scores on the E.P.V.T. (r = 0.25 significant beyond 0.001 level). In the middle-class area, social class is more strongly associated with high E.P.V.T. scores (r = 0.34 significant beyond 0.001 level) than is the Maternal Index (r = 0.23 significant beyond 0.01 level). This is yet another example of the weaker discriminating power of the Index in the middle-class area.

So far then, we have considered the relationships between social class, family size, ordinal position and the Index to the ability scores of the children in each area at the ages of five and 6+ years of age. We will now consider the relationships between the sex of the child and ability scores and the relationship between the sex of the child and the Maternal Index of Communication and Control. There is no significant relationship between the sex of the child and any ability test in either area except in the case of the E.P.V.T. score for working-class boys. In the working-class area boys show a tendency to attain higher E.P.V.T. scores than girls (r = 0.15 significant beyond 0.05 level) and this relationship remains when we control for the size of the family. Perhaps the most interesting finding arises out of the examination of the relationship between the sex of the child and the Maternal Index score. In the working-class area the score on the Maternal Index shows no significant relationship with the sex of the child. However in the middle-class area there is a relationship between the Maternal Index score and the sex of the child. In this area, Low Maternal Index scores are relatively strongly associated with girls (r = 0.30 significant beyond the 0.001 level). Middle-class mothers show a strong tendency to alter their patterns of communication and control according to the sex of the child. In particular middle-class mothers are more likely to use coercive and imperative modes of control and explain *less* to the girl than to the boy. No such difference between the sexes was found in procedures of Maternal Communication and Control in the working-class area. *To our knowledge this is the first time that research has revealed the class patterning of sex differences in processes of communication and control.*

101

Up till now we have presented findings showing the relationships between aspects of the family and the ability and W.I.S.C. scores of the children in the two areas. In order to show the power of the Maternal Index we shall turn to the mothers' relationship with the school and to the teachers' estimates of the children's future school career. These relationships have been picked out *not* because they represent the *only* associations between the Index and variables external to the family (a future monograph will explore all the associations between the Maternal Index and school variables) but only to give examples of the power of the Maternal Communication variable.

We wanted to obtain some indication of how the social classes differed in the degree to which they saw both the school and the home as jointly involved in the behaviour of the children. We constructed a closed schedule which was given during the first maternal interview in which the mother was asked to indicate for each of 22 different areas of the child's behaviour whether she thought that each was mainly the concern of the mother alone, or the school alone, or whether *both* the home and the school were jointly involved. (See Appendix V for the schedule.) After the mother had filled in this schedule the mother was again presented with the list of 22 different areas of the child's behaviour and she was asked to tick the areas where she thought there might be a possible disagreement between herself and the school. (Appendix IV). We refer to these schedules as the 'boundary' schedule and the 'disagreement' schedule. In the working-class area a high score on the Maternal Index is relatively strongly associated with mothers who indicate that they favour a joint position with the school across the 22 different areas of the child's behaviour. Mothers in the working-class area who have Low Index scores are less likely to favour a joint position with the school as far as these items of their child's behaviour is concerned ($r = 0.33$ significant beyond 0.001 level). In the middle-class area there is no significant correlation between high scores on the Index and mothers who favour a joint position with the school. Indeed in the middle-class area the correlation is negative although not significant ($r = -0.16$). The differential effect of the Maternal Index in the two areas is highly significant beyond the 0.001 level. Once more we find that the Index works in the working-class area but not in the middle-class area. Now let us turn to the 'disagreements' schedule. We were able to distinguish within the different areas of the child's behaviour, areas of behaviour which represented behaviours of the child in the home rather than behaviours of the child at school (see Appendix IV). We then correlated the Maternal Index score with the *number* of items in the home area, which the mother ticked as indicating a source of possible disagreement with the school. A high score on the Index, in the working-class area, is related to a mother who sees *few* disagreements between herself and the school on behaviours of the child which fall within the home area. Whereas a low score on the Index, in the working-class area, is related to a mother

102

who sees a greater number of disagreements between herself and the school on behaviours of the child which fall within the home area (r = 0.25 significant beyond the 0.001 level). In the middle-class area there is *no* correlation between the Index score and the number of disagreements which fall within the home area (r = 0.07). Although the differential effect of the Index in the two areas on this 'disagreement' schedule is not significant, the fact that the correlation is 0.25 in the working-class area and 0.07 in the middle-class area shows that there is indeed a strong tendency towards a differential effect. We should perhaps add that there is no significant correlation between mothers who favour a joint position with the school and the number of disagreements between school and home in those areas of the child's behaviour which occur within the home (r = 0.08). Thus the correlation established between each of these schedules and the Index does not arise because of a correlation between the two schedules.

The final result we wish to present concerns the relationship between social class, the Maternal Index score and the W.I.S.C. to the teachers' estimates of how well the child would fare in his future school career. After the children had completed their first and second year in the infant school the teacher in charge of each year completed a questionnaire which was concerned with the child's behaviour during each year. The findings of this questionnaire will be published separately in a future Sociological Research Unit monograph. Here we shall concern ourselves only with one of the questions which the teachers answered. This question simply asked the teacher to assess each child on a three point scale in terms of how well she thought each child would do at school. The number of schools involved in this analysis is ten schools out of our total of 13 in the working-class area. The teachers' ratings of the three schools in Control Group 2 (see Introduction) could not be used because the mothers of the children were not interviewed. In the middle-class area all the five schools are in the sample. It will be remembered that the research in the middle-class area was always one year behind the research in the working-class area and that the middle-class children were given the shortened version of the W.I.S.C. As we have as yet not transformed the scores of the shortened version of the W.I.S.C. into I.Q. points and also because we have not completed the analysis of the teachers' questionnaires for the first *and* second year of the middle-class children's school life, we shall present the findings *only in terms of the first and second year of infant school life in the working-class.* We chose to correlate the teacher's estimates with the W.I.S.C. because this is a more reliable test than the ability tests given when the children were five years of age and because the W.I.S.C. was given to the working-class children approximately three months before the teachers filled up the questionnaire at the end of the school year.

In the working-class area the correlation between parental social class and the teachers' estimate of the child's future school career is 0.25, that is the higher the social class of the parents in that area the more likely the teachers thought the child would do well. The correlation between the Maternal Index score and the teachers' estimate of the child's future school career is however 0.33, that is, High Maternal Index scores are associated with a good school prognosis. Notice that at the end of the child's first year at school there is a *higher* correlation between the Index and the teacher's estimates than between social class and the teacher's estimates. Now let us look at the relationship between social class and the Maternal Index score and the teachers' estimates of the child's future school career at the end of the *second* year. We find that the social class correlation remains almost unchanged. It rose from 0.25 at the end of the first year to only 0.28 at the end of the second year. However, the correlation between the Maternal Index score and a favourable teacher's estimate rose from 0.33 at the end of the first year to *0.42* at the end of the second year.

Now if we examine the relationship between high W.I.S.C. scores of the child and a favourable teacher's estimate of the child's future school career we find, as we would expect, a very high correlation. At the end of the child's first year, the correlation between a high W.I.S.C. score and a favourable teacher's estimate is 0.49. This correlation rises to 0.58 at the end of the child's second year. It would seem, then, that the most powerful effect upon the teacher's estimate is the child's W.I.S.C. score which of course the teachers did not know. However, before we leap too readily to conclusions we should bear in mind the strong correlation between the W.I.S.C. score and the Maternal Index ($r = 0.38$). Let us explore this relation between the Maternal Index, social class and the W.I.S.C. score to the teacher's estimate a little further. If we control for social class, that is if we remove the effect of social class on the Maternal Index score, the W.I.S.C. scores and the teachers' estimates, we find that all the correlations are reduced only slightly by almost equivalent amounts. Now if we take the further step of controlling for both social class *and* the W.I.S.C. scores we find that there is *no* significant correlation left between the Maternal Index score and the teachers' favourable estimate of the child's future school career at the end of the first year. However when we consider the teachers' estimates at the end of the *second year* we find that despite controlling for *both* social class and the W.I.S.C. score there is still a small but significant correlation left between the Maternal Index and a favourable teacher's estimate ($r = 0.22$ significant beyond the 0.01 level). *Thus over time the Maternal Index score has an effect independent of parental social class and the W.I.S.C. score upon these children who receive favourable teachers' estimates.*

Before commencing the discussion of these results it might be helpful if we summarised very generally the main findings.

1 The correlation between the Maternal Index of Communication and Control and social class for the whole sample is 0.57.

2 In the working-class area the Maternal Index score is more strongly associated than is parental social class with the three ability tests. In the middle-class area the position is reversed with the correlation between the three ability tests and social class much higher than the correlations between the tests and the Index.

3 In the *working-class* area the correlation between the W.I.S.C. scores (given to the children when they were six years of age) and the Index is higher (0.38) than the correlation with social class (0.25).

4 There is no relationship in either the middle-class or the working-class area, between family size or ordinal position and the score on the Index. There is a relatively strong relation (0.30) between the Index scores and the sex of the child in the middle-class area. In the middle-class area and *only* in the middle-class area, girls are more likely to be treated coercively by their mothers and have less explained to them than boys.

5 Only in the working-class area is there a tendency for family size (large) to be related to the ability and W.I.S.C. scores of the children.

6 There is some indication that younger children in both middle-class and working-class areas may score higher on the E.P.V.T.

7 High scores on the Maternal Index in the working-class area is associated with mothers who favour a joint relationship with the school across a range of behaviours of the child. High scores on the Index is associated with mothers who are less likely to disagree with the school over areas of the child's behaviour which fall within the home domain. The Maternal Index score of mothers in the middle-class areas is not related to scores on either the 'boundary' or 'disagreement' schedules.

8 In the working-class area, a high score on the Maternal Index is more highly correlated with favourable teachers' estimates of the child's future career than is the social class position of the child's parents. The correlation between high scores on the Maternal Index and favourable teachers' estimates increases between the first and second teachers' estimate, whereas the correlation between social class and the first and second teacher estimates remains unchanged.

9 In general the Maternal Index of Communication and Control is more sensitive (in the sense that it is correlated with a range of variables internal and external to the family) in the working-class area than in the middle-class area.

Discussion of the Findings

The first major point of interest is the strength of the association for the whole sample between the social class ratings of the parents and the score on the Index of Communication and Control (r = 0.57). There can be little doubt that according to the mothers' reports the social classes differ radically in their use of language for purposes of explanation and control,

105

(see also Bernstein and Henderson, 1968) and in the willingness of mothers to respond to communications initiated by their children. The Index gives some indication of the frequency, range and quality of the mothers' reported communications to children. It is a matter of some importance that the mother's score on this Index is not related to the size of the family, or to the ordinal position of the child. From a common sense point of view this does seem a curious result, but it suggests that the Index is measuring an orientation towards the *relevance* of language, which is independent of the number of children in the family and the child's ordinal position.

We shall consider first, differences *between* the middle-class and the working-class area in the size of the correlations between the three ability scores and parental social class position. Secondly, we shall discuss the social class correlations within each area with the Matrices and the verbal tests. Thirdly, we shall consider the correlations between the Maternal Index and the three ability tests in the two areas.

Although there is a marked difference in the size of the social class correlation with the ability scores in the two areas, this difference in the size of the correlation can be almost wholly explained in terms of the difference in the variance within social class in the two areas. The social class variance in the middle-class area is significantly greater than the social class variance in the working-class area. (See Appendix I) by Brandis W. Thus the social class correlations with the two verbal tests are much higher in the middle-class area. (We shall consider the social class correlations with the Matrices in the next step of the discussion.)

If we now look at the social class correlations with the ability tests *within* each area we note the following:

(1) Within the middle-class area the social class correlation with the Matrices is lower than the correlations between social class and the verbal tests. Indeed there is a significant difference between the class correlations with the Matrices and the E.P.V.T. (beyond 0.05 level). The test which correlates most highly with social class is the E.P.V.T.

(2) In the working-class area there is little difference in the size of the correlations between the ability tests and social class. There is some suggestion that in the working-class area there is a reversal in the rank order of the correlations compared to the rank order in the middle-class area. In the working-class area the lowest class correlation is with the E.P.V.T. and the highest is with the Matrices. We must be cautious, however, for the differences in size of the social class correlations with each of the ability tests is very small.

We offer the following explanation for these apparently curious findings. The Matrices test is less culture bound than the two verbal tests, so that given non-deprived environments we could expect a lower correlation between the Matrices score and social class in the middle-class area. The two verbal tests are much more affected by culture and particularly by the cultural emphasis upon verbally realised meanings. We have good reason to believe that in the middle-class, children with an initially favourable genetic endowment, are developed through a form of socialisation which emphasises the linguistic categorising and elaborating of relationships. We found that the social class variance is significantly greater in the middle-class area than in the working-class area, so that in the middle-class area compared to the working-class area, there is a more extended class hierarchy. We suggest than an emphasis upon linguistic aspects of socialisation follows this more extended class hierarchy. As a result, within the middle-class area the social class correlations with the verbal ability tests and, in particular, with the E.P.V.T. are much higher than the social class correlations with the less culture bound Matrices test.

As the differences in the size of the social class correlations with the ability tests in the working-class area are so small it is unjustified to offer much comment. Yet despite the increased social class variance in the middle-class area the class/Matrices correlation is small rather than high and in the working-class area despite the *reduced* social class variance the class/Matrices correlation is the highest of the three ability tests. The low class correlation with the Matrices in the middle-class area is understandable as the Matrices, relative to the verbal tests, is less culture bound. On the other hand, there is some reason to believe that where the environment is very impoverished, the Matrices scores may be depressed rather more than the scores on verbal tests (Shuey, 1966). The working-class area does contain a segment which is considerably impoverished. It is possible, then, that within the working-class area there is a range of class-linked environments from relatively normal to acutely impoverished. It is this range which may be responsible for the relatively higher Matrices correlation. We are suggesting that there is a degree of curvilinearity in the relationship between social class and the Matrices test.

In the middle-class area all the ability test correlations with the Maternal Index score are very much lower than the ability correlations with social class. This is because the Maternal Index variance in the middle-class area is relatively small; the Index has little discriminating power within the middle-class area. On the other hand, in the working-class area, *all* the ability test correlations with the Maternal Index score are higher than the ability test correlations with social class. This is because there is much greater variance in the Maternal Index scores than in parental social class position. Thus in the working-class area, the Maternal Index score is capable of producing finer discriminations between families than is the social class Index. We consider that the score on the Maternal Index in the working-class area is reflecting differences between families in their emphasis upon aspects of linguistic socialisation. In order to discriminate between families in the middle-class area, we shall have to develop a much more sensitive Index of Communication and Control.

107

Before leaving this discussion of the differences between the social class and Maternal Index score correlations with the ability tests, we should like to draw attention to the cultural influence upon the E.P.V.T.

(1) The Maternal Index score in the working-class area is more highly correlated with the E.P.V.T. than with the other two ability tests.

(2) Although all correlations between the Maternal Index score and the ability test scores, in the middle-class area, *fall* relative to the three ability test correlations with social class, the fall in the Maternal Index score correlation with the E.P.V.T. (relative to the class correlation) is *less* than in the case of the two other tests.

(3) The E.P.V.T. is the only test of the three which correlates with the ordinal position within the family in *both* areas, younger children in larger families attaining higher scores.

It would appear then that the scores on the E.P.V.T. are subject to considerable environmental influence. However, it is the E.P.V.T. rather than the Crichton or Matrices which shows the most consistent correlations with both the verbal and the performance scales of the W.I.S.C.

Our conclusion is that the differences in the ability test correlations with social class in the two areas can be explained in terms of the differences in the social class variance in the middle-class and the working-class area. We have explained the higher correlations of the verbal tests, particularly the E.P.V.T. with social class in the middle-class area, in terms of a class-linked emphasis upon cognitive aspects of linguistic socialisation. We suggest that there is a degree of curvilinearity in the relationship between social class and the Matrices scores, and we account for the differential effect of the Maternal Index score *between* the two areas in terms of the greater power of the Maternal Index to discriminate between families within the working-class area.

The Index score is a specific consequence of parental social class position and is at the same time a sensitive measure of sub-cultural differences within the working-class area. It is likely that both the social class and the Maternal Index correlations are higher with the W.I.S.C. than they are with the three ability tests given to the children when they were five years of age because the W.I.S.C. is a more reliable test. It could also be that the Index correlation with the W.I.S.C. is higher than with the ability tests because the early patterns of communication and control between mother and child have consequences for the child's later development. We should not leave out of account the effect of the one year at school upon the children's W.I.S.C. scores. However, the effect of the school upon the W.I.S.C. scores of the children would, on the whole, lower the correlation with the Maternal Index score, unless all the mothers with low Index scores had children in the most unfavourable schools, and mothers with high Maternal Index scores had children in the most favourable schools. We know that such a distribution does not occur in our sample. It is a matter of considerable interest that there is still a highly significant correlation (r = 0.22) between the Maternal Index and the W.I.S.C. scores, even when the effects of social class are completely removed from this relationship.

So far our discussion has concentrated upon the higher correlations between the Index scores of mothers and the working-class children's ability and W.I.S.C. scores. However, it could bè argued that these correlations arise out of the intelligence of either mothef or child or out of their interaction. For example, a bright child might be more likely to initiate communications with his mother and encourage and reward her replies to him, whereas dull children may not be so stimulating to some mothers. On the other hand, bright mothers might talk and explain more to their children than less bright mothers. We can offer no unequivocal answer to this problem as we have as yet no estimate of parental intelligence, but an attempt to clarify the problem will be made in the second part of this discussion.

The research suggests that the transfer of skills as measured by ability tests, especially verbal tests, may well be mediated through processes of communication and control.

We are now going to consider, somewhat briefly in this monograph, the sex typed patterns of communication and control that we find within the middle-class. This is important for a number of quite different reasons. It gives us reason to believe that the middle-class mothers were not simply reporting on what they took to be socially acceptable behaviours. The fact that the middle-class mothers reported that they were more coercive with their girls and explained less to them, indicates that where it was appropriate they did give other than conventional replies. The norms which do exist would have led us to believe that girls are treated less coercively than boys. So that the first significance of the sex typing of patterns of communication and control within the middle-class is that it gives us more confidence in these mothers' reports. The relationship between a low Maternal Communication Index score and the depressed form-class scores of the middle-class girls also gives us grounds for confidence in the mothers' reports.

In as much as the middle-class mothers say that they are more coercive with their girls and explain less to them, it would seem that the girls, relative to the boys, are socialised, initially, into a more submissive role and that their cognitive perspective is limited. The early socialisation of the middle-class girls may well be influenced by the mothers' perception of the *difference* between the boy's and girl's future adult role. Our data *at this stage of the analysis* does not allow us to say more than to stress the need for more extensive sociological enquiries into the different forms of sex typing in the social classes and their consequences. It may well be, that the cognitive orientation of girls and their relationships to authority, owe much to their initial family socialisation. Whilst our research shows sex typing of communication and control in the middle-class, it does not reveal such a form of sex typing within the working-class. Clearly this is not to say that sex typing within the working-class does not occur, nor it is to say that it does not occur through different forms of communication. It is only to say that our methods of analysis and research did not reveal such differences between boys and girls of this age within the working-class. This may be because the working-class mothers in our sample *as a whole* were more coercive and were less likely to offer explanations. On the other hand, the middle-class mothers revealed a greater range of alternatives in response to the same questions and therefore their choice is likely to be more child-specific. Questions which release responses which allow us to show sex typing in one social class may not be appropriate for revealing sex typing in another social class. We believe that further analysis of the data will throw more light upon the different ways in which mothers of different social class position discriminate between boys and girls.

We will now consider the social class and Index correlation with aspects of the mothers' relationships to the school and the child's performance at school. We find that in the middle-class area, there is no significant correlation between social class or the Maternal Index score and the replies to the 'boundary' schedule area. This lack of correlation indicates that mothers *as a whole* in the middle-class area see that the behaviours of the child (at least the range which were given in the 'boundary' schedule) are also the concern of the school. In the same way, and for the same reason, there is no correlation in the middle-class area between social class or the Index scores *and* potential disagreements between the parents and the school over aspects of the child's behaviour which fall within the domain of the home. In the working-class area, as we have seen, there are significant correlations between social class and the Index scores and the 'boundary' and 'disagreement' schedule. Again the Index score correlations are much higher than the correlations with social class. Thus a low score on the Index in the working-class area is associated with a mother who does not favour a joint position with the school over the behaviour of her child and who is likely to see disagreements between the school and herself over areas of the child's behaviour which fall within the domain of the home. Here we have an example of how processes of communication and control *within* the family relate to the mother's response to the school. *The lower the score on the Maternal Index in the working-class area the more likely that powerful forms of cultural discontinuity exist between the family and the school.*

Finally, we shall discuss what we consider to be one of the most important findings we have reported: the relationship in the working-class area between the social class position of the parents and the maternal Index score to the teachers' estimates of the children's future school career. The correlation between the Index score and favourable teachers' estimates is important because here we are examining the relationship between the mother's reports on what she *says* she does when the child is under five-years of age and the teacher's evaluations of the child when he or she is aged six and seven years.

The results show that in the working-class area at both six and seven-years of age a favourable teacher's estimate of the child's future school career is more highly correlated with the Index score of the mother than with the family's social class position. Indeed the correlation between the social class position of the family and a favourable teacher's estimate hardly rises between the end of the child's first year at school and the end of the child's second year. Whereas the correlation between high scores on the Maternal Index and a favourable teacher's estimate *rises* dramatically in the same period of time. A High Maternal Index score is related to the child receiving a favourable teacher's estimate of his future school career even when we have controlled for *both* the child's W.I.S.C. score and the family's social class position. This finding is of importance because it gives us greater confidence in the validity of the Index score, for the correlation suggests that the working-class mother's report on what she *says* she does, bears a relation to what she *actually* does. It also suggests that communication processes between mother and child may well have consequences for the child's future development.

In order to obtain a closer understanding of class related differences in patterns of communication and control, we shall have to broaden the terms of this discussion. So far, it seems that the Maternal Index score is a more sensitive discriminator in the working-class area, for only in the working-class area does the score relate both to the children's ability test scores and to the mother's relation to the school. In Henderson's chapter, there is a suggestion that a component of the Index (the verbal interaction and avoidance schedules) relates to the speech of the middle-class children but less to the speech of the working-class children. We are now going to include findings from other aspects of the research, in order to obtain a more detailed picture of the origins and consequences of the Maternal Index score.

Social Class, Maternal Index Score, Ability, Language use and Education

We shall consider in this section, social class differences in the effects of (1) the children's ability test scores, and (2) the Maternal Index score, upon the mother's general orientation towards the education of the child and upon aspects of the children's use of language. The findings are based upon an intensive analysis of a sub-sample of 99 middle-class children and 130 working-class children and a sub-sample of 96 middle-class and 94

111

working-class mothers. We are fully aware that the analysis to follow raises complex statistical issues which we have, as yet, not attempted to solve. We are presenting this analysis because it appears to open up a fruitful area of enquiry highly pertinent to this monograph.

Bernstein gave an account in the introduction, of the first interview of the mothers which took place before the children went to school in the September. In the interview, we were concerned to examine the mother's general orientation towards the education of her child as this would be revealed through talking about the following areas:-

(1) Reading
(2) Play and Toys
(3) Relationship to the school
(4) Failures in the child's learning at school

The full details of this interview will be written up in a future monograph entitled 'Social Class and the Infant School Child' by Mrs. Jean Jones. Here we shall simply report how the mothers' responses in these four areas relate to the ability of her child and to the Maternal Index of Communication and Control.

There were 27 significant correlations for *both* social class groups between the Maternal Index score and the mother's general orientation towards the education of her child. High scores on the Maternal Index are in general related to:-

(1) Mothers who prepare their child for school in a number of ways, who see play as having an educational value and who, in an unstructured context, stress the explorative use of toys.
(2) Mothers who read frequently to the child and to library membership of mother or child, or both.
(3) Mothers who see failure in learning as arising out of a complex of factors and who take positive steps to help the child.
(4) Mothers who are favourably disposed towards teachers, who see the relation between teacher and child as non-hierarchical and who, in general, cooperate with the school.

High scores on the Maternal Index then, indicate a favourable orientation towards the education of the child. When we examine the social class distribution of these 27 correlations we find that 17 of them occur *within* the middle-class and only 10 *within* the working class group. So it seems that the Maternal Index is more sensitive within the middle-class sample. When we consider the correlations with the ability test scores of the child, the picture is somewhat different.

The reader will remember that the children were given three ability tests at five years of age: English Version of the Peabody Picture Vocabulary Test (E.V.P.T.), Crichton Scale and the Progressive Matrices. We shall report the number of significant correlations between the three tests combined and the four areas. The total number of correlations with the three ability tests and the variables within four areas for the two social classes is 35. However, 24 of these occur *within* the working-class group and only 11 within the middle-class group. On the whole, working-class mothers with *high* ability children, tend to have a more favourable orientation towards the education of the child, whereas *within* the middle-class group, favourable orientation of the mothers is *less* related to tne ability of the child.

The following table sets out these results:

	Favourable Orientations		Correlations
	M.C.	W.C.	
Maternal Index	17	10	27
Ability Tests (3)	11 (8)	24 (15)	35 (23)

Favourable orientations towards the child's education are more related to the Maternal Index score in the middle-class group *and are more related to the ability of the child in the working-class group.* The figures in brackets refer to correlations which are ability test specific.

Now we shall turn to the relationships between the ability of the child, the Maternal Index, and aspects of the children's speech. At the moment we are only able to consider the choices within the nominal group. This group is important, for the choices within it control the verbal realisation of categories, the ascribing of attributes to categories and the qualifications and elaboration of categories (see Henderson's chapter). The full account of the children's choices within the nominal group will appear in a future monograph by Mr. Peter Hawkins.

In general, there are very few significant correlations between the Maternal Index and the nature of the child's choices within the nominal group. Yet within the middle-class sample, high Maternal Index scores are related to the use of role playing speech, the use of relational elements (the boy's father, John's ball, etc.) and the use of somewhat rare prepositions of manner. Within the working-class, high Maternal Index scores are related only to exophoric usage, i.e. where the referent of the statement is implied e.g. 'that's flying'.

We will now consider the relationships between the ability of the child and aspects of nominal group usage. In general, there are far more correlations in *both* social classes between the ability of the child and aspects of nominal group usage than between the Maternal Index and nominal group usage. Yet it is the case that the higher the social class, the *less* the ability of the child is related to aspects of nominal group usage. In other words, elaboration of the nominal group *within* the middle-class children is less related to their ability scores than is the case with working-class children. Low ability working-class children are also more likely to use imperatives and exophorics. This is not the case with low ability middle-class children. When middle-class and working-class children are matched for ability, it is

113

likely that the speech of the middle-class children will be more elaborated and more specific. This will be particularly true in the case of high ability pre-school children.

The following table sets out these findings:

	Nominal Group Usage	
	M.C.	W.C.
Maternal Index	more	less
Ability Tests	less	more

Now let us put all these findings together, first of all to see the effect of the ability of the child and secondly, to see the effect of the Maternal Index, in the two social classes.

	Ability Scores	
	M.C.	W.C.
Maternal Index	–	+
Favourable Educational Orientations	less	more
Nominal Group Usage	less	more

It appears from the above table that high ability in working-class children is related to the mother's pattern of communication and control, to her favourable educational orientation and to developed nominal group usage in the children. In the middle-class group the ability of the child is much less related to these three variables. This would seem to indicate that in the working-class the bright child is in a generally favourable position, whereas in the middle-class, relative to the working-class, all children, irrespective of their ability, are in a *more* favourable position in relation to their future education.

	Maternal Index	
	M.C.	W.C.
Ability Tests	–	+
Favourable Educational Orientation	more	less
Nominal Group Usage	more	less

On the other hand, the Maternal Index is not related to the ability of the child in the middle-class group, but is, *relative to the working-class group*, more strongly associated with mothers who have favourable educational orientations and is more related to developed nominal group usage in the children. In the working-class group, the Maternal Index is associated with the children's ability but is, *relative* to the middle-class group, much less related to the other two variables.

114

The crucial issue now is whether in the working-class group the bright child, initially, has this potential or whether this is developed through the mother's pattern of communication and control? In the working-class, does the mother *respond* to her bright child in such a way that a benign circle is set up? Another way of putting the issue, is to suggest, that in the middle-class it is what is in, or not in, the mother that counts; whereas in the working-class it is, what is in or not in, the child's head that counts. It is difficult indeed, to sort out what is essentially a chicken and egg problem but we can try and push this issue a little further.

Earlier we said that within the middle-class group there were 11 correlations between the combined ability tests and a favourable educational orientation as revealed by the mothers' responses in the four areas: preparation of the child, play/toys, failures in the child's learning and the mothers' relationships to the school. In the working-class group we said there were 24 correlations between the ability tests and the mothers' responses within these four areas. The table below shows the number of significant correlations between each ability test and the four areas.

	E.P.V.T.	Crichton	Matrices
M.C. (four areas combined)	3(3)	2(2)	6(3)
W.C. (four areas combined)	8(5)	10(7)	6(3)

If we consider the figures in brackets, which refer to correlations which *are specific* to a test, (that is they do *not* overlap with correlations with any other test) then we can see that the responses of working-class mothers relative to middle-class mothers are much more influenced by the child's ability in the verbal area. In the middle-class, there are 5 correlations within the verbal tests *total* and variables within the four areas whilst in the working-class group, there are 12 correlations between the verbal tests and variables within the four areas. If we can interpret the verbal tests as indicating what the child says and the Matrices as indicating what the child does, (the level of his cognitive/manipulative skill) then it would appear that the working-class mother forms her judgement of the child's ability *more* in terms of what he says, than in terms of what he does. Whereas, the middle-class mother forms her judgement equally in terms of both what he says and does. This makes sense when we consider that the bright working-class child with high language ability is likely to stand out among his siblings and peers and therefore, is perhaps, treated differently because he, himself, stimulates his mother.

In the middle-class group, 2 out of 3 correlations with the Matrices test are negative; that is the mother's responses are affected if her child's Matrices score is *low*. Thus if the child's Matrices score is *low* then the middle-class mother is more likely to prepare her child for attentiveness, ('Do what the teacher says'), and she will prepare this child very much in terms of what she takes to be the school's requirements. The middle-class

115

mother may well consider that a low level of manipulative/construction skill in her child, particularly when there are few compensating signs in the language area, is an indication that her child is less bright and so she will perhaps, prepare this child for school in a way rather different from a bright child. The middle-class mother acts with reference to both high ability (verbal tests) and low ability children (non-verbal tests); whereas the working-class mother tends to act with reference *only* to high verbal ability.

As there is no correlation between the Maternal Index score *within* the middle-class group, and the ability tests, it is unlikely that the middle-class mother would act to depress the child's ability scores, it may be appropriate to infer that it is something already *in the child* which is affecting the behaviour of the mother. On this basis we are prepared to argue that in the working-class it is the child with originally a high potential who calls out of the mother a favourable orientation towards education and which affects her pattern of communication and control. In other words, within the working-class, some encouraging mothers have brighter children because the children are born bright; whereas in the middle-class, the mother is concerned for both bright and less bright children. The crucial person in the middle-class, on this analysis, appears to be the mother, whereas the crucial person in the working-class appears to be the child — the high verbal ability child. Clearly much more analysis of our data is required in order to substantiate our argument, but the first analysis points to this conclusion.

We will now summarise the major findings and inferences:

1 Ability Test Scores

Within the middle-class group relative to the working-class group:-
   (a) High ability scores of the children are *less* related to mothers who have a favourable orientation towards the education of the child.
   (b) High ability scores of the children are *less* related to elaboration of the children's speech.
   (c) High ability scores are *not* related to the Maternal Index score.

Within the working-class group relative to the middle-class group:-
   (a) High ability scores of the children are *more* related to mothers who have a favourable orientation towards the education of the child.
   (b) High ability scores of the children are *more* related to elaboration of the children's speech.
   (c) High ability scores *are* related to the Maternal Index score.

2 Maternal Index Score

Within the middle-class group, high Maternal Index scores are *more* related than, in the working-class group, to the mothers who have a favourable orientation towards the education of the child. High Maternal Index scores of middle-class mothers are related to signs of elaborated speech in the children.

We therefore suggested the following:-

(a) Middle-class children, when compared with working-class children, on the basis of ability, are likely to show a more developed use of language. It is likely that high ability working-class children will be penalised *more* in such comparisons because of class differences in the quality of the mothers' communications. The middle-class bright child has more to work on than the working-class bright child. Indeed, insofar as it is the school which provides (or should provide) an appropriate context for language development, the middle-class child is singularly fortunate, as the schools he goes to are likely to be materially and educationally better. (See Newsom 'Half our Future' and Plowden, 'Children and their Primary Schools').

(b) Because in the middle-class, high Maternal Index scores are associated, relative to the working-class group, with a more favourable orientation to education and because high Maternal Index scores are associated with signs of elaboration in the children's speech, we believe (bearing in mind (1) that in the middle-class, the crucial person is the mother, whereas in the working-class the crucial person is the child – the high ability child. There are indications (which require more delicate analysis) that the working-class mother appears to be acting only with reference to a child who initially has a high potential. Thus, *less* able working-class children receive less stimulation and support in their education than do less able middle-class children.

(c) The Middle-class mother is more likely to base her estimates of her child's ability in terms of what the child says *and* what the child does (cognitive manipulative skills). The working-class mother is more likely to base her estimates on what the child says (verbal ability). *Thus the middle-class mother in comparison with the working-class mother is sensitive, responds to a wider range of behaviour offered by the child.*

(d) There is one more example of the independence within the middle-class of patterns of communication and control from the ability of the child. The patterns of communication and control vary with the *sex* of the child *only* within the middle-class. A girl in this social class tends to be socialised into a more submissive role and her cognitive horizon tends to be more limited.

(e) Whilst it appears to be the case that working-class mothers tend to act with reference to high ability children, there is one important exception. Within the working-class group, high Maternal Index scores are related to the children who at seven years of age receive

117

from the teacher a favourable school prognosis.* This relationship between High Maternal Index scores and a favourable teacher's estimate of the child's future school career, holds even when the children's W.I.S.C. scores are partialled out of this relationship. We also know that working-class mothers with high Index scores, are on the whole, more prepared to cooperate with the school. So, whilst it is the case that there is an indication that working-class. mothers tend to act with reference to the high ability child, it is also the case that *in terms of the teacher's assessment of the child's future school career, working-class mothers with high Index scores may bring about beneficial consequences for the children because of their more generally cooperative relationship with the school.*

The argument should not be taken to mean that maternal patterns of communication and control do *not* affect ability or that they do *not* affect the speech of the child. It would also be very inappropriate to consider that the *sole* origin of relatively developed patterns of communication of the working-class mother is the brightness of her child. At the moment, the data points to this as one factor.†

We have already mentioned (e) as an example of the working-class mother's response which is relatively independent of her child's ability. We have one other important example of the independence of the score on the Maternal Index. Within the working-class, there is a significant relationship between a component of the Maternal Index, (the verbal interaction and 'avoidance' schedules) and mothers who rank highly 'to find out about things', (Bernstein and Young, 1967). There is also a significant correlation of 0.25 between mothers who rank in this way and the children's W.I.S.C. score at six years of age. Even when we partial out (control for) the child's W.I.S.C. score, a small but, significant, correlation remains between high scores on this component of the Maternal Index and mothers who rank highly 'to find out about things', as one of six uses of toys. These are two

---

*This analysis has not yet been carried out in the case of the middle-class sample.

† It is important to clarify this argument further, for as it stands it could be misleading. It should *not* be taken to support the view that we should develop more efficient screening procedures to identify the "bright" working – class child. The argument simply points to a *specific* child in the working class who may be a potential source of stimulation to the mother. It may equally be the case that the same child or a similar sib is (or has been) regarded favourably by the teacher who tells the mother of his possibilities. In this way the school is responsible for the particular and specific relationship that the mother may *only* have to this child in her family. Our data at this stage (further data may *extend, modify* or *change* the argument) points to some discrimination in favour of the working – class child who is thought to be "bright". It also points to the possibility that the working – class mother, relative to the middle – class mother, may fail to take steps which would encourage the attainments of other children who are not so labelled. We should also point out that there are factors other than the narrow mother – child inter-action which lead to the description of a child as "bright". We are grateful to Miss Elizabeth McGovern, S.R.U., for drawing attention to these points.

118

examples which suggest that high scores are relatively independent of the child's ability. These examples then, do not point to the child as stimulius but to the mother.

We might now argue that high Index scores in the working-class group are partly reflections of the brightness (potential) of the mother. Because the mean Index score in the working-class is 94 S.D. 24, whilst the mean Index score in the middle-class is 127 S.D. 16 there is probably a massive difference in the contents of these mothers' speech. As a result, the speech of working-class five-year-old children, relative to the speech of middle-class five-year-old children, is less elaborated through the mothers' communications. Differences in language as between working-class children are then more likely to arise out of differences in their potential. The bright working-class child possibly is able to respond to the school and make *more* from the limited language offered by the mother than the less able working-class child. All middle-class children are offered a more elaborate pattern of communication, which in turn develops aspects of their speech, with the consequence that the relation between the ability test scores of the children and these children's speech is *less* extensive than in the case of working-class children.*

The development and expression of the potential of mother and child in the working-class is limited by the sub-culturally determined process of communication. We now have the possibility that in the working-class, what matters is the *high* potential of mother *or* child. But this potential is realised through a sub-culture which does not *develop* forms of language use and which does not develop cognitive skills favourable to the child's education. In the working-class then, it may be the case that *only* bright mothers have a favourable orientation towards their child's education, but even in this case it is *not* made *substantive* in their behaviour. Whereas, because of the sub-culture, in the middle-class, *all* the mothers have orientations which are favourable towards their child's education and *all* mothers to different degrees, *are able to adopt appropriate means* in developing an environment which is favourable to their child's education.

Further analyses of the data may help us to clarify this complex issue.

*There is a contradiction here between these inferences and D. Henderson's finding that *only* in the middle-class is the ability of the child related to his form class usage. We are as yet unaware of the specific relationships between certain linguistic choices and measured ability. Therefore it may well be the case that when different linguistic variables form the basis of the correlations with measured ability we may find a different pattern of significance. We should therefore treat this argument in the text with some reservations. However, we should point out the well established fact that the relationship between measured ability and educational attainment is less direct in the case of the middle-class child, whereas the relationship between measured ability and educational attainment in the case of the working-class child is much more direct.

119

Conclusion

Our discussion has really been in two stages. In the first stage, we reported results obtained from a sample which was drawn from the geographical areas. We felt justified in describing these areas as working-class and middle-class, because of the high correlation (0.74) between area and its social class composition. We showed that for the whole sample, the social classes differed radically in their patterns of communication and control. We also showed that the Maternal Index of Communication and Control correlated with a greater number of variables, both family and school, in the working-class area. We concluded this stage of the discussion with the statement that in the working-class area, where the mother's attained low Index scores, *powerful forms of cultural discontinuity existed between the home and the school, and the ability of the child is depressed.* However, we felt that we could hardly leave the matter there, because the findings suggested that the Maternal Index score discriminated only within the working-class area. The data did not allow us to consider the origins of the Maternal Index score and the different consequences of the scores.

We decided to broaden the terms of the discussion in order to examine in some detail, the different effects and possibly different origins, of high scores on the Index. In order to do this, we drew our data from intensive analyses of middle-class and working-class sub-samples, which have been used for the main analysis of the children's speech and for the analysis of the first maternal interview. We were then able to consider a wider range of variables. This analysis revealed the relative importance of the Maternal Index of Communication and Control *within* the middle-class group and the relative importance of high ability scores of the children within the working-class group. We shall develop further analyses to test the implications. It is important to point out that the mean Maternal Index score in the middle-class group is 127 S.D. 16. Whereas the mean Maternal Index score in the working-class group is 94 S.D. 24. If it is the case that the working-class mother is responding to her bright child, then there is still a massive social class difference in the quality of her response.

If we ask what it is that the Maternal Index is measuring then we might say that it is measuring the degree of openness of the communications between mother and child. Where the Maternal Index score is high the child's world is expanding and open, when the score is low, his world is limited and closed. Where the Maternal Index score is high, the relationship between home and school is open to reciprocal influence, where the score is low there is insulation and often hostility between home and school. It may also be the case that both *high and low* Maternal Index scores can have deleterious consequences for the children.

Processes of communication and control are realisations of cultures or sub-cultures and are the means of their transmission. Considerable sensitivity is required of those who wish to modify them. This is not to be taken as an argument to leave the situation as it is, rather it is to warn against a bull in a china shop approach. Much can be done through the development of nursery schools and in working out an approach so that the school can become neither a bridge nor a ferry but a growing point in the consciousness of the community. Even more can be done to ensure that the teacher's core responsibility, the transfer of skills and sensitivities, can be effectively carried out. For in the final count, it is *what* goes on and *how* it goes on in the *school* that matters. Educational visitors, teacher/social workers, although highly relevant, are no substitute for constant appraisal of both the methods we are using, and the culture and organisation of the school.

The Wider Implications

The findings reported in this chapter although of considerable significance do not give us a warrant for generalisation. We have no means of relating the communication variables to higher order social structure variables, for in the first maternal questionnaire, we asked no questions which would help us to relate the patterns of communication and control to the character of the role system of the family and to its controlling values. Neither have we information which would allow us to identify the variables external to the family which influence its values, role system and subsequent patterns of communication and control. At the moment then, we have only an Index of very limited aspects of communication and control which we cannot relate to higher order social structure variables. It is possible that the findings of the second maternal questionnaire given two years later, may help us to move beyond the limitations of our initial approach. The schedules which formed the basis of the Index were not originally conceived with the developed Index in mind. It was the analysis of Brandis which made possible the integration of the schedules into a composite Index.

We are very conscious that our study is concerned only with the mother and only in terms of *her* response to the child. We need to have also, information about the conditions and contexts which regulate how, when and where the *child* initiates verbal interactions with the *parents*. It is also the case that we have ignored extra-verbal aspects of communication and we have sampled only a very narrow range of communication contexts. We have no measures of differences in personality between mothers and between children. Perhaps, the most glaring omission is the neglect of the father. This is not because we under-value the significance of the father but our budget did not permit any further increase in the size of the sample. To have included the fathers would have meant that we would have had to reduce the number of families and this in turn would have prevented us from carrying out a number of statistical analyses of patterns of interaction among the variables.

121

What we have been examining is the sub-cultural consequences of differences in social class position as these consequences shape the cognitive development of children and the mother's relationship to the school. In turn the cognitive socialisation of the child and the mother's perception of her relationship to the school initially shape (with other factors) the child's role as pupil. But these two important components of the pupil's role are aspects of the sub-culture made substantive. Indeed the cognitive socialisation of the child and the home's relation to the school are indices of more general relationships between the family and the wider social structure. If we can show the process where-by the sub-culture is made substantive in these two areas, we have the beginnings of a means to explain the social origins of educability.

Other studies have shown the importance of family size, birth order, the literate status of the home, the aspirations of the parents, the 'encouraging' mother and achievement motivation to educational success and failure. Continuity and discontinuity between home and school has been examined at a more sociological level in terms of adequacy or inadequacy in the children's learning of appropriate social roles, or in terms of discrepancies between the values of the home/community and those of the school, or in terms of the differences between social class groups in their ability to exert pressure upon the school. But we need to know *how* adequate and inadequate pupil roles are learned and *how* values are transmitted. What we have tried to do is to go behind these factors to a study of the processes they pre-suppose. What we have presented here is only a beginning.

Social class groups are by no means homogeneous and attempts to show correlations between the members of such groups and children's responsiveness to school will inevitably leave much of the variance unexplained. From the point of view of the influence of the *family* upon children's responsiveness to school, we need to start, not with social class as our independent variable, but with an understanding of those variables which we believe to control the social antecedents of educability. We can then assess the degree to which the presence or absence of those controlling variables coincide with the social class divisions we construct. If our theory of the social antecedents of educability is sensitive, then we could explain both the homogeneity *and* the heterogeneity within the social class groups. The Index of Communication and Control is a short step in this direction for it discriminates within working-class sub-cultures as we have shown here and elsewhere. (Bernstein and Young, 1967). If this Index could be made both more extensive and more delicate then we might be able to measure with greater sensitivity, differences within and between social class groups.

In all work concerned with comparative socialisation within a society, there is always a danger that the differences such studies reveal will be transformed into statements of 'better' or 'worse'. This is particularly the case where the groups involved are social class groups and the socialisation is into the school. Once such judgements are made, implicitly or explicitly, that one form of socialisation is 'better' than another it is but a short step to consider how we can transform the 'worse' into the 'better'. Can we make the working-class as the middle-class? This question is based upon the dubious premise that socialisation within contemporary middle-class strata and the education we offer in the schools represents the acme of three quarters of a million years of civilisation. It equally as inevitably leads on to a view of the child as a deficit system, his parents as inadequate and their culture as deprived. The very form our research takes reinforces this view. It shows nearly always what the middle-class *do* and what the working-class do *not* do in relation to the middle-class.

Perhaps one of the major functions of such comparative studies of socialisation is to make us face, and challenge rather than accept, the ideological assumptions. If this is done we may be able to objectify the assumptions of our own socialisation and to examine critically the criteria of educability we have taken over. In other words the question which stands over and beyond the particulars of class socialisation is that of the forms, contents and gaols of education, for these define what is appropriate to the role of pupil and teacher. Once we raise this question we are less concerned with the differential strengths and weaknesses of class socialisation and far more concerned with the forces which make for rigidity in the educational system and a sense of its inevitability.

REFERENCES

Bernstein, B. & Henderson, D. (1969) Social Class Differences in the relevance of Language to Socialisation, *Sociology, 3,* 1.

Bernstein, B. & Young, D. (1967) Social Class Differences in Conceptions of the Uses of Toys, *Sociology, 1,* 2.

Shuey, A. M. (1966) *Testing Negro Intelligence,* 2nd. Edition, Social Science Press.

For a general evaluation of child rearing and socialisation with particular reference to modern Britain, see Klein J. (1965) *Samples of British Culture,* Vol. I & II, Routledge & Kegan Paul: and for empirical descriptive surveys, see Newson, E. & Newson, J. (1963) *Infant Care in an Urban Community,* Allen & Unwin, and Newson, E. & Newson, J. (1968) *Four-Years-Old in an Urban Community,* Allen & Unwin.

Overall Correlations between Maternal Index of Communication
and Control and School Indices

	Working Class Area (n = 196)			Middle Class Area (n = 141)		
	1.	2.	3.	1.	2.	3
1. Maternal I.C.C.	1.000			1.000		
2. Boundary (school area)	.343***	1.000		-.022	1.000	
3. Disagreements in home area	.293***	.130	1.000	.112	.019	1.000

Significance levels obtained using the r to z transformation

* = p $\langle$ .05   ** = p $\langle$ .01   *** = p $\langle$ .001

Sample: Working-Class and Middle-Class Area. (Mothers)

Working-Class Area

	Total	West Indian	Remainder	Faulty Tapes	Final Sample
Total children	320				
Twins	6				
Total Mothers	314	22	292		
3 Control 11 Schools *	72	5	67		
10 Remaining Schools	242	17	225		
Refused Interview	13	3	10		
fully interviewed	229	14	215	11	204

* Only background data collected

Middle-Class Area

	Total	West Indian	Remainder	Faulty Tapes	Final Sample
Total children	153				
Twins	3				
Total Mothers	150	1	149		
Refused Interview	-	-	-		
Fully interviewed	150	1	149	2	147

Sample Children of Mothers with full Maternal Interview Data

Working-Class Area

	Total	Refused IQ	IQ Sample	Refused W.I.S.C.	W.I.S.C. Sample
Original Sample	204				
Drop out from school	5				
up to Autumn 64 (IQ)	199	3	196		
Drop out from school	22	-	22		
up to Autumn 65 (W.I.S.C.)	177	3	174	-	174

Middle-Class Area

	Total	Refused IQ	IQ Sample
School - Autumn 65 (IQ)	147	6	141

TOTAL

	Total	Refused IQ	IQ Sample
School - First Term (IQ)	346	9	337

125

Overall Correlations between Family Background Variables,
Maternal Index of Communication and Control, and
Ability Scores

Working
Class Area
(n = 196)

	1.	2.	3.	4.	5.	6.	7.	8.
1. Social Class Index I	1.000							
2. Family Size	.195**	1.000						
3. Ordinal Position	.154**	(.859)	1.000					
4. Sex	.021	.028	-.033	1.000				
5. Maternal Index of Comm-unication & Control	.417***	.111	.116	-.009	1.000			
6. Matrices	.188**	.183*	.107	.070	.181*	1.000		
7. Crichton	.170*	.221**	.125	.068	.256***	(.331)	1.000	
8. E.P.V.T.	.137	.199**	.064	.156*	.246***	(.366)	(.552)	1.000

Social Class[1] partialled out from Matrix (with Family Size[2]
partialled out from Ordinal Position[3])

	2.1	(3.2)1	4.1	5.1	6.1	7.1	8.1
2.1 Family Size	1.000						
(3.2).1 Ordinal Position within Family Size	-	1.000					
4.1 Sex	.024	-.110	1.000				
5.1 Maternal Index of Comm-unication & Control	.034	.056	.000	1.000			
6.1 Matrices	.152*	-.094	.067	.115	1.000		
7.1 Crichton	.195**	-.123	.065	.207**	(.309)	1.000	
8.1 E.P.V.T.	.177*	-.208**	.154*	.210**	(.350)	(.542)	1.000

Significance levels obtained using the r to z transformation

$* = p < .05$ $** = p < .01$ $*** = p < .001$

Overall Correlations between Family Background Variables,
Maternal Index of Communication and Control, and
Ability Scores

**Middle
Class Area
(n = 141)**

	1.	2.	3.	4.	5.	6.	7.	8.
1. Social Class Index I	1.000							
2. Family Size	.118	1.000						
3. Ordinal Position	.116	(.709)	1.000					
4. Sex	.140	-.006	.067	1.000				
5. Maternal Index of Comm- unication & Control	.340***	-.039	.024	.300***	1.000			
6. Matrices	.109	.008	-.044	-.014	.055	1.000		
7. Crichton	.295***	.130	.111	.010	.107	(.163)	1.000	
8. E.P.V.T.	.337***	.137	-.018	.067	.230**	(.160)	(.579)	1.000

Social Class[1] partialled out from Matrix (with Family Size[2]
partialled out from Ordinal Position[3])

	2.1	(3.2).1	4.1	5.1	6.1	7.1	8.1
2.1 Family Size	1.000						
(3.2)1. Ordinal Position with- in Family Size	-	1.000					
4.1 Sex	-.023	098	1.000				
5.1 Maternal Index of Com- munication & Control	-.085	.067	.271**	1.000			
6.1 Matrices	-.005	-.075	-.012	.019	1.000		
7.1 Crichton	.100	.019	.010	.008	(.138)	1.000	
8.1 E.P.V.T.	.104	-.184*	.062	.130	(.151)	(.533)	1.000

Significance levels obtained using the r to z transformation

* = p <.05 ** = p <.01 *** = p <.001

Working Class Area (n = 162): Pooled Within-Schools Correlations

	1.	2.	3.	4.	5.
1. Social Class Index I	1.000				
2. Maternal Index of Communication & Control	.413***	1.000			
3. W.I.S.C.	.247**	.375***	1.000		
4. Teachers' Rating Future School Career 1	.252**	.330***	.492***	1.000	
5. Teachers' Rating Future School Career 2	.277***	.414***	.579***	.568***	1.000

Social Class partialled out from Matrix

	2.1	3.1	4.1	5.1
2.1 Maternal Index of Communication & Control	1.000			
3.1 W.I.S.C.	.309***	1.000		
4.1 Teachers' Rating Future School Career 1	.256**	.458***	1.000	
5.1 Teachers' Rating Future School Career 2	.343***	.550***	.535***	1.000

Social Class[1] and W.I.S.C.[3] partialled out from Matrix

	2.13	4.13	5.13
2.13 Maternal Index of Communication & Control	1.000		
4.13 Teachers Rating Future School Career 1	.136	1.000	
5.13 Teachers Rating Future School Career 2	.218**	.385***	1.000

Significance levels obtained using the r to z transformation

$* = p < .05$ $** = p < .01$ $*** = p < .001$

Working Class Area (n = 174)

Overall Correlations of Social Class and Maternal Index of Communication & Control with W.I.S.C.

	1.	2.	2.1
1. Social Class Index 1	1.000		
2. Maternal Index of Communication & Control	.392***	1.000	
3. W.I.S.C. Total	..279***	.358***	.282***
3a W.I.S.C. Verbal	.231**	.295***	.229**
3b W.I.S.C. Performance	.266***	.341***	.267***

Significance levels obtained using the r to z transformation

$* = p < .05$ $** = p < .01$ $*** = p < .001$

Correlations between the Components of the
Index of Communication and Control and the
Main Variables for the Combined Areas.
(n = 337)

	Toys	Avoidance	Verbal Interaction	Reasoning	Punishment	Mothers I.C.C.
Social Class 1	.404	.358	.366	.362	.365	.566
Sex	.063	.035	.018	.145	.094	.105
Family Size	.194	.134	.028	.072	-.002	.127
Ordinal Position	.193	.167	.059	.074	-.021	.144
Matrices	.215	.166	.074	.160	.149	.232
Crichton	.199	.195	.156	.172	.190	.282
E.P.V.T.	.247	.272	.168	.193	.240	.346
Disagreements (home)	.231	.236	.282	.146	.211	.350
School (Boundary)	.233	.150	.197	.193	.078	.255
Sex in the Two Areas						
Working Class (n = 196)	.016	-.094	-.052	.073	.047	-.009
Middle Class (n = 141)	.141	.228	.097	.217	.168	.300
Social Class and I.Q. in the W.C. Area (n = 174)						
Social Class 1	.261	.185	.298	.282	.206	.392
W.I.S.C.Verbal	.179	.198	.156	.226	.175	.295
W.I.S.C. Performance	.251	.271	.115	.176	.247	.341
Total W.I.S.C.	.239	.256	.157	.228	.242	.358

129

APPENDIX I

AN
INDEX OF SOCIAL CLASS
by W. Brandis

The Problem

The social background of a child is often represented only by the occupational status of the father, but the occupational status of the mother and the educational status of both parents might also be important components of what is understood by family social status. The Brown-Spearman coefficient of reliability shows that, given a consistent level of correlation between items, a scale becomes more reliable as the number of items entering into its construction increases. It follows that an index made up of four items is more reliable than an index which uses one item only, so long as those items have an equal or near-equal status in relation to the dimension being measured.

The problem is whether the occupational status and educational level of each parent can be measured on a level high enough to construct a scale which is more than nominal-ordinal in character. Each item, however scored, will be measuring a continuum of social status. The question is whether the scoring of the item can represent spaces on the continuum accurately, and so achieve the measurement level of an interval scale. The short answer seems to be 'No'.

Occupational Status is measured by the position that a job occupies on the Hall-Jones Scale, which is essentially an ordinal scale based initially on clusters of ranks ([1]). Yet the very fact that the initial rankings of occupational status did cluster indicates that the scale has achieved a level of measurement higher than bare ordinality (i.e. simple rank ordering). As so often happens in the behavioural sciences, the scale in question occupies a level somewhere between ordinal and interval measurement, having surpassed the first but not achieved the second. Three possible alternative courses of action follow, each with substantial reservations.

1 Treat occupational status as an ordinal scale, thus losing little information and being secure in the use of non-parametric models of analysis. But in so doing, the important quality of additivity is denied, so that the variable cannot be combined with one or more other variables to form a larger, more reliable, scale. Moreover, non-parametric models are less highly developed than their parametric counterpart, particularly

with reference to 'statistical' — as against physical — control procedures, so that analysis must remain relatively simple (and relatively uncontrolled) in design.

2 Circumvent the problem by imposing a two-category solution. Any ordinal or nominal scale may be re-grouped into two categories, 'A' and 'not-A', which while apparently nominal in character, may be treated as an interval scale. The precondition that the ratio between intervals must be known has not been violated when there is only one interval, whatever the state of our knowledge about its size. However, on an extended ordinal or marginally higher order scale such as the Hall-Jones, raising the measurement level to interval scaling in this way does result in a very real loss of information. 'Respectability' may thus be achieved at a considerable price ([2]).

3 Assume that the ratios of the intervals between ordinal categories is known. This assumption is most economically made by reference to the classic notion of 'equal-appearing intervals', where each interval is assumed to be precisely equivalent to every other interval on the scale. Highly developed parametric models may be used in analysis, and no information is lost through this procedure. But the more the actual Hall-Jones Scale deviates from the assumption of equal intervals, the more misleading any results derived from its use. Despite the unknown size of this reservation, the effective paralysis generated by the first alternative and the loss of information following the second has led us to adopt this third course ([3]).

The Hall-Jones occupational status of the Father was coded by reference to his present job, or, if unemployed, to his last job. As might be expected, however, most mothers were unemployed and had not been employed for some time. If they were working, it is likely that a primary criterion for job-choice would be its lack of dissonance with the role of mother, rather than any consideration allied to social status. It would therefore be reasonable to infer that present employment constitutes a somewhat unreliable index of occupational status, and gives only an occasional indication of the stylistic and aspirational network to which the mother, by virtue of her occupational history, has been exposed or considers salient. Equally, her last job before marriage or child-birth may well have been primarily chosen for financial reasons, so that the same reservations would apply. Accordingly, mothers' occupational status refers to whatever job she has held that occupies the highest position on the Hall-Jones Scale. The distribution, mean, and standard deviation for both variables as follows:-

	1	2	3	4	5	6	7	N	x	S
HJ Father	29	34	55	70	136	85	42	451	4.49	1.63
HJ Mother	1	10	43	214	31	86	66	451	4.74	1.34

131

Educational Status again, presents little difficulty on an ordinal level, but unlike its occupational counterpart, has no established measurement convention which may be described as ordinal-approaching-interval. In this situation, a solution requires the use of external criteria. Categories of educational background may be compared with each other both in terms of relative size, and in terms of the mean Hall-Jones Score of the appropriate parent:

	Father		*Mother*	
	N	xHJ	N	xHJ
Sec. Mod: left 15 or earlier	302	5.21	295	5.29
Sec. Mod: left 16 or later	18	3.22	6	3.83
Lower Professional or Commercial Qualifications	30	3.47	39	3.80
Grammar: left 16 or earlier	47	3.60	56	3.96
Grammar: left 17 or later	35	2.54	44	3.55
Higher Professional or University Qualifications	19	1.74	11	2.73

Among both fathers and mothers, there is a clear gap in occupational status between the minimally educated Secondary Modern Early Leavers and the rest. The remainder are surprisingly homogenous, with the exception only of the very few who achieved a University level of education. Moreover, no less than two-thirds of each parent fall into the lowest educational category, so that anything more than a two-point scale would be highly skewed indeed. The scale of educational status, then, adopts a two-category solution:-

	more than minimal = 1	minimal = 2	N	x	S
Edn Father	149	302	451	1.67	.47
Edn Mother	156	295	451	1.65	.48

Construction of the Index

The correlations between the four items are as follows:-

Item	1.	2.	3.	4.
1. HJ Father	1.000			
2. HJ Mother	+.513	1.000		
3. Edn Father	+.626	+.442	1.000	
4. Edn Mother	+.517	+.559	+.599	1.000

A factor analysis produced one general (social class) factor ([4]), accounting for .657 of the matrix variance. Since the factor loadings refer to standardised variables, the relative weight given to each item in constructing an index must equal the factor loading divided by the item's standard deviation.

Item	Factor Loading	$\dfrac{FL}{s}$ = relative weight
1. HJ Father	.821	.51
2. HJ Mother	.766	.57
3. Edn Father	.827	1.75
4. Edn Mother	.827	1.74

It is clear that the two educational items should have approximately three times the weight of occupational status, so the formula for constructing a social class score becomes quite simply:-

Index of Social Class = (HJ Father + HJ Mother) + 3 (Edn Father + Edn Mother). This summed score, which has a potential range of 0–18, was compressed into a ten-point scale 0–9, such that for either parent one interval on the social class Index represents one interval on the HJ scale or one-third of an interval on the scale of educational status.

Since any factor loading in an orthogonal factor structure is also the correlation of the item with the factor, it is appropriate to compare the original factor loadings with the part-whole correlations of each item with the final Index (r_{iT}):

Item	Factor Loading	r_{iT}
1. HJ Father	.821	.835
2. HJ Mother	.766	.760
3. Edn Father	.827	.813
4. Edn Mother	.827	.814

Despite a slightly increased weight given to the occupational status of the father at the expense of the remaining items, the correspondence between the initial factor loadings and the final part-whole correlations is remarkably high.

Description of the Index Categories

In order to obtain some perspective of the social class index, it is instructive to observe the item means within each of the index arrays:

Index of Social Class Category	HJ Father $\bar{x}$ (Mode)	HJ Mother $\bar{x}$ (Mode)	Edn Father $\bar{x}$	Edn Mother $\bar{x}$	N
0	1.00 (1)	1.80 (2)	1.00	1.00	5
1	1.44 (1)	3.09 (3)	1.00	1.00	32
2	2.80 (3)	3.74 (4)	1.00	1.00	50
3	3.49 (4)	4.00 (4)	1.07	1.21	29
4	3.76 (4)	3.88 (4)	1.52	1.44	25
5	4.53 (5)	4.27 (4)	1.77	1.43	44
6	4.82 (5)	4.35 (4)	1.88	1.92	85
7	5.33 (5)	5.34 (6)	1.97	2.00	92
8	5.59 (6)	6.48 (7)	2.00	2.00	77
9	7.00 (7)	7.00 (7)	2.00	2.00	12

Alternatively, the index arrays may be described by the proportion of 'pure' Middle or Working Class parents within them, where MC = HJ 1, 2, 3, 4 + Edn 1, and WC = HJ 5, 6, 7 + Edn 2:

Index of Social Class	Both MC	One MC	One MC, One WC	One WC	Both WC	'Neither pure'	'N'
0	5 (1.00)						5
1	32 (1.00)						32
2	49 (.98)	1 (.02)					50
3	14 (.48)	15 (.52)					29
4		21 (.84)	1 (.04)			3 (.12)	25
5			23 (.52)	5 (.11)		16 (.36)	44
6			6 (.07)	61 (.72)		18 (.21)	85
7				50 (.54)	42 (.46)		92
8					77 (1.00)		77
9					12 (1.00)		12

These two tables suggest category descriptions on a dimension which runs from totally Middle Class to totally Working Class:

Social Class Index	Category Description	N
0–2	Totally MC	87
3	Predominantly MC	29
4	Marginally MC	25
5	Mixed	44
6	Marginally WC	85
7	Predominantly WC	92
8–9	Totally WC	89

Validity and Reliability

An external criterion may be used to indicate the relative validities of the index against the single items of which it is composed. The total sample is, in fact, two separate samples, one drawn from a pre-established Working Class area and one from a Middle Class area. Taking area from which the sample is drawn as the independent variable, and the four items plus the index as dependent variables, the correlation ratio E^2 states the proportion of variance accounted for in the dependent social class variables by area. The square root of the correlation ratio is directly analogous to the product-moment correlation coefficient r, and in the limiting two-sample case, it is equal to r.

Dependent Variable	$E = r$
Social Class Index	.742
1. HJ Father	.661
2. HJ Mother	.549
3. Edn Father	.625
4. Edn Mother	.585

As expected, the index is much more closely related to area than the separate items are, indicating that social class is more validly measured by the former. It is of interest to note that HJ Father is clearly the most important single item, so that its increased weight in the index relative to the factor loadings is apparently justified.

To assess the reliability of the Social Class Index, a measure involving a direct estimate of true and error variances is required. The split-half method does this, but it is criticised on the grounds that it overestimates reliability by incorporating correlated (time-specific) errors. It is likely, however, that where the questions are of an objective, externally verifiable nature, such as kind of job and educational background, correlated errors of this kind should rarely appear in the data. The requirement of 'equivalence' between the two tests in split-half reliability does not appear to be violated if Father's occupational level plus Mother's educational level are combined against Mother's occupational level plus Father's educational level. The application of the Brown-Spearman formula to the correlation between these two split-halves produces a reliability coefficient of .875

An Alternative Index

The assumption that the seven categories on the Hall-Jones Scale are divided by equal intervals is perhaps too glib. As there are grounds for supposing that the interval between categories 4 and 5 may be 'larger' than other intervals, the HJ scale has been recast into four categories (with equal-appearing intervals between them) in such a way that the distinction between 4 and 5 assumes a relatively greater importance.

| | | Father | | Mother | |
Hall-Jones Categories	New Score	N	x HJ	N	x HJ
1,2,3 Upper Middle	1	118	2.22	54	2.78
4 Lower Middle	2	70	4.00	214	4.00
5 Upper Working	3	136	5.00	31	5.00
6,7 Lower Working	4	127	6.33	152	6.43

The education level of the parents remains as a two-category scale, but the few parents who stayed at Secondary Modern after their 16th birthdays have been included among the 'minimally educated'. A second index on an 11-point scale has been constructed from these reorganised variables such that Social Class Index II = (Ocpnl. Status Father + Mother) + 2 (Ednl Status Father + Mother).

Despite the markedly increased bimodality of the second index, and an expectation of some curvilinearity in its relationship with the first index, the (linear) correlation between the two indices, $r_{12} = + .978$, is extraordinarily high. Not surprisingly, the correlation between area from

135

which sample was drawn and the second index is virtually the same as that between area and the first index, the former being marginally higher at $E = r = + .746$.

It thus becomes a matter of indifference whether the first or second index is chosen to measure social class. In general, however, it has been decided to use the first index to measure social class within this Research.

Notes

(1) 'Social Mobility in Britain' ed D.V. Glass: Pt I Sec. II, 'The Social Grading of Occupations' by O. A. Moser and J. R. Hall.

(2) It is difficult to resist the temptation to treat the two-category solutions as a distinct classificatory — i.e. nominal — system, implying homogeneity within the categories and heterogeneity between them. But if the regrouped scale was initially ordinal-approaching-interval, then the final categories should display a high degree of internal heterogeneity. Now if the regrouped variable is in turn broken against a second variable which correlates highly with it, then sub-categories of 'A' — or of 'not-A' will not be equal on the first variable, even though they bear the same name 'A' (or 'not-A'). If the second variable is also a regrouped two-category scale, then the error would simply be compounded. To use such a cross-break as a control system for one or the other variable may be followed by highly misleading conclusions, for it is not possible to estimate the contribution made by the internal heterogeneity of the 'control' category. The combination of two or more associated scales into an 'index', where the index categories are treated as (quasi-ordinal) complex nominal groups defined by the unique combination of component scale categories, may be designated the 'nominal-ordinal solution'. It is unsatisfactory because the ordinality is all too often left unclear and therefore unexploited, and because the use of 'nominal' combinations can in this context be so distinctly misleading.

(3) Standard textbooks which discuss the problem of measurement level include Q. McNemar 'Psychological Statistics' (1962) Ch. 19, pp 374—5, and S. Siegel 'Non-Parametric Statistics' (1956), Ch. 3.

(4) Using Hendrikson-White factor analysis program on the IBM 7090 at Imperial College. An important feature of that program is the use of varimax rotation to arrive at eventually oblique solutions, which can in turn be factor analysed to extract higher order factors. In this particular analysis, however, no rotation was possible as only one factor has originally been extracted.

APPENDIX II

A MEASURE OF THE MOTHER'S ORIENTATION TOWARDS COMMUNICATION AND CONTROL
by W. Brandis

Introduction

It has been suggested that interaction within different social strata is governed by different characteristic role structures[1]. A typical speech model is seen as interwoven with the mechanics of social control, which in turn are contingent on a typical role structure. The familial speech model, being both the product and a transmitter of the family structure, might be considered as the dynamic agent between social status and intelligence. This theoretical stand suggests that any empirical attempt to trace the process by which social background is translated into intelligence must be concerned with the measurement of communication and control procedures within the family.

Five indices of Mother's Orientation Towards Communication and Control

A questionnaire given to mothers elicited a mixture of closed and open responses about the orientation of the mother towards communication and control. Four schedules have been chosen for this analysis on the grounds that the data is the most systematically ordered, and that they bear most directly on the central concern of this paper.

1 *Schedule E* samples the universe of responses available to the mother when the child asks difficult questions.

SCHEDULE E

Besides everyday questions, children often ask about things which are difficult to explain to a child. What do you find you mostly do?

	Never	Sometimes	Often
1. Try and change the subject.			
2. Make up something until they are older.			
3. Tell them a little bit until they ask again.			
4. Tell him/her as much as you can.			
5. Tell them to ask Daddy.			

137

In order to construct an index measuring the mother's disposition to answer difficult questions asked by the child, it is necessary to assume additivity between the items. Since interval scaling is a prerequisite for additivity, the convention of assuming equal intervals between the categories of a (simple) ordinal-approaching-interval scale has been followed. It has been assumed, therefore, that the interval between 'never' and 'sometimes' is precisely equal to that between 'sometimes' and 'often'.

Clearly, the response to items 3 and 4 indicates the mother's disposition to answer difficult questions, while the responses to the other three items indicates her disposition not to answer them. A composite scale, therefore, requires items 3 and 4 to be scored in a direction opposite to the remaining items. The further consideration that item 4 is much stronger in content than item 3 suggested that the former should receive twice the weighting of the latter. An 'Avoidance' Index measuring the mother's disposition to answer, or avoid answering, difficult questions from the child, was, therefore, constructed as follows: $2 (E/4) + E/3 - (E/1 + E/2 + E/5)$.

In order to assess whether the construction of the scale is consistent with the pattern of interrelationships between items, the schedule was factor analysed.[2] Two factors, accounting for .300 and .226 of the matrix variance, were extracted and rotated to an oblique solution:-

	Unrotated (orthogonal) Factors		Rotated Oblique Factors	
Item	Factor 1	Factor 2	Factor 1	Factor 2
E/4	.37	-.62	.22	-.68
E/3	.05	-.81	-.14	-.80
E/5	-.59	-.03	-.58	.09
E/2	-.67	-.04	-.66	.10
E/1	-.75	-.30	-.80	-.14

Thus two quite distinct factors emerge, items 1, 2 and 5 constituting a separate factor from items 3 and 4. Somewhat disturbingly, the correlation between the oblique factors is only -.03. However, a factor analysis of the two oblique factors did produce a general factor, which, translated into original variable factor loadings, presents a solution fairly consistent with the constructed Avoidance Index:-

Item	Standard Deviation	Level 2 Factor Loadings	FL/S
E/4	.58	.65	1.11
E/3	.60	.47	.79
E/5	.59	-.48	-.82
E/2	.70	-.55	-.78
E/1	.60	-.47	-.79

The factor loadings divided by the item standard deviations indicate that item 4 should receive a greater weight than the other four items, although not as much as twice the weight. It was decided, however, that the way in which the Avoidance Index was originally constructed did not do great violence to the second level factor. The scale is, therefore, retained in its original form.

The reliability of the Avoidance Index may be estimated by the split-half method. In general, this method tends to overestimate reliability by incorporating correlated time-specific errors due to response set. However, the reversal of items should deal effectively with the latter problem, and the heterogeneity of the items will result in split-halves not strictly parallel, so tending to underestimate reliability. In the hope that the tendency to overestimate in general and to underestimate in this particular would balance out (but also suspecting a net underestimate) items $1 + 4$ were correlated with items $2 + 3 + 5$, all weighted as before. The application of the Brown-Spearman formula to the split-half correlation produced a reliability coefficient of .430. If this estimate of reliability is unbiased, then more than half the variance in the Avoidance Index is error variance.

2 *Schedule F* samples the situations in which interaction with the child is not a defining activity, but could emerge because the child 'applies' to initiate it.

SCHEDULE F

As well as asking questions children also chatter quite a lot. I'd like you to imagine yourself in the following situations and say what you usually do.

	Tell him/her to stop	*Tell him/her to wait*	*Talk to him/her quickly*	*Chat with him/her*
1. You are working around the house.				
2. You are walking along the street.				
3. You are trying to relax.				
4. You are talking to your husband.				
5. You are in a shop.				
6. You are in a bus or tube.				
7. At meal-times.				

The need to assume an interval level of measurement in order to build a scale now becomes distinctly awkward. However, in the absence of evidence to the contrary, it has again been decided to assume equal intervals between the ordered categories. The seven items were given equal weight and then summed into a scale (the Verbal Interaction Index) measuring the mother's disposition to continue a verbal interaction initiated by the child.

As with the previous schedule, a factor analysis was subsequently performed on the seven items([2]). The proposition under examination was simply whether the items in Schedule F constitute a general factor. Two factors, accounting for .254 and .174 of the variance respectively, were extracted, rotated to an eventually oblique solution, and in turn factor analysed to produce one 'second level' factor. The first unrotated factor in the initial analysis was indeed a general factor, as was the factor extracted on the second level, but the factor loadings of the latter were rather more consistent with each other in size than they had been in the first (original) general factor.

Item	1st Unrotated Factor	2nd Level Factor	Standard Deviation	FL(1)/S	FL(2)/S
F/1	.43	.42	.90	.48	.46
F/2	.68	.53	.72	.95	.73
F/3	.34	.50	1.11	.31	.45
F/4	.37	.57	.57	.65	1.00
F/5	.47	.52	.71	.66	.72
F/6	.71	.57	.68	1.07	.83
F/7	.39	.33	1.21	.32	.28

As an added complication, there is a tendency for large standard deviations to be associated with smaller factor loadings. Dividing the latter by the former thus accentuates the differences between the actual weights which should be given to the items. However, a general verbal interaction factor does underpin the correlation matrix, albeit weakly, so the original Chatter Index was retained.

The comments on the reliability of the Avoidance Index apply in every detail to the Chatter Index except that there is no reversal of items and, therefore, no counter to response set. Items 2 + 4 + 7 were correlated with items 1 + 3 + 5 + 6 to produce a reliability coefficient via the Brown-Spearman formula of ·466.

3 *The Control Questionnaire* samples behavioural problem situations initiated by the child, and asks the mother to relate what her response to the child would be.

Apart from answering questions, mothers have to deal with problems children set them. Here are some every day problems which mothers have told us come up with children:

140

1. Supposing you thought it was time . . . . . went to bed, but he/she started to cry because he/she wanted to watch something on T. V. What would you say or do?
2. What would you say or do if . . . . . wasn't watching what he/she was doing and spilt tea over the table-cloth?
   Probe. What would you do or say if he/she took no notice?
3. What would you do if . . . . . brought you a bunch of flowers, and you found out that he/she had got them from a neighbour's garden?
4. Supposing your husband forgot to bring . . . . a present that he'd promised and he/she wouldn't talk to his/her father all day. What would you say or do?
5. Imagine . . . . . has started school, and one day he/she says "I don't want to go to school today" but he's/she's not ill or anything, but just doesn't want to go to school. What would you say or do?
   Probe: If after that . . . . . began crying and saying "I don't want to go"
6. Imagine . . . . . had been out shopping with you and when you got home you found he'd/she'd picking up something from one of the counters without you noticing. What would you say or do?

In all there are nine control situations, comprising of six initially posited situations, with three persisting after the mother's first control response. Each response was coded within a complex scheme involving 87 categories of Control Strategy (Avoidance, Punishment, Support and Reparation), Appeals (Positional and Personal), Rationale (permutations of positional-personal and universal-specific within a framework of both description and justification), Blame and Involvement. The score in each category consists of the number of control situations in which that category of response appears, making a total possible score of nine. The scaling, which might be described as 'weak' ratio, was again treated as interval.

Given an elaborate coding scheme of open data such as this, it is not altogether surprising that the modal response in 82 of the 87 categories is zero.* However, some 40 of the least skewed items were selected for a factor analysis. As was to be expected, there was no clear factorial structure underlying the data beyond a general dimension. This dimension was a hypothesised bipolar factor dominated by punishment at one end and child-orientated personal appeals at the other. Repeating the factor analysis with the 17 least skewed items produced a general 'response' factor and substantially the same bipolar factor. As there is some

*The coding frame was devised from a theory of social control which stressed the symbolic component of control, and which allowed for a wide range of possibilities. It was not expected that there would be an even distribution of responses across *all* the coding categories. The coding frame may be obtained from the Sociological Research Unit.

uncertainty about the relative weights of the two poles because of the operation of other items, two separate indices were constructed: (1) a Punishment Index, with (a) Physical Punishment obtaining a double weight to (b) Verbal Punishment and (c) Categoric Repetition (i.e. statements of the order 'I'd make him do it'); (2) a Child-oriented Reasoning Index, with equal weight given to (a) Simple Cognitive Child-oriented Personal Appeals, (b) Complex Cognitive Child-oriented Personal Appeals, (c) Cognitive-Affective Child-oriented Personal Appeals, and (d) Recognition of the child's intent. It was felt that since like responses may have represented alternatives to the respondents, the calculation of split-half reliabilities was rendered inappropriate.

4 *Schedule D* samples the functions that toys may be thought to perform:

SCHEDULE D

Here are some ideas about what toys are for. Please put 1 for the use which you think is most important, a 2 for the next most important, and so on until 6 for the least important.

A. To keep the children amused by themselves.

B. So that they can play with other children.

C. So that they can find out about things.

D. To free the mother so that she can do other things.

E. To help them when they go to school.

F. To show that mother cares when she has been away.

The primary interest in this schedule focusses on the cognitive child-oriented item 'C' against the instrumental mother-oriented item 'D'. After some consideration, item 'F' (affective mother-oriented) was defined as operating on the same general level as item 'D'. The research orientation towards pitting item 'C' against 'D' and 'F' is reflected in the average ranks given to the items by the sample:

Item	Average Ranks
C	2.06
E	3.07
A	3.23
B	3.37
F	4.40
D	4.87

Since the respondents were asked to rank items, rather than rate the importance of each item independently, two serious problems emerge. The cognitive child-oriented to instrumental/affective mother-oriented dimension posited above certainly appears theoretically plausible, but (1) what kind of test can be used to decide that this dimension rather than any other theoretically plausible dimension is the major underlying factor, and (2) how can an index be constructed? No solution is yet seen to the first problem.

However, an index has been constructed by counting the number of independent rank deviations from 'C' ranked 1st plus 'F' and 'D' (irrespective of order) ranked 5th and 6th; thus the highest possible number of such deviations is 11, where 'C' would be ranked 6th and 'F' and 'D' (any order) 1st and 2nd. However, even given that these are the appropriate items with the appropriate (equal) weights, two very substantial reservations must be made about this index: (1) that, as might be inferred from the average ranks of the items, it is highly skewed, and (2) that the proposed assumption of equal intervals is distinctly questionable.

A General Index of Mother's Orientation towards Communication and Control

The different forms of the data on which the five indices are based may be summarised as below:

Index (Source)	Whether Closed Data	Whether Independent Items
Avoidance (Schedule E)	Yes	Yes
Verbal Interaction (Schedule F)	Yes	Yes
Punishment (Control Schedule)	No	Uncertain
Child Oriented Reasoning (Control Schedule)		
Toys (Schedule D)	Yes	No

The formal status of the indices clearly differs considerably. Two of them are based on open data (the Control Schedule), with the independent status of items somewhat uncertain. A third index, though closed, has item scores which are logically dependent on the other item scores (Schedule D). Split-half reliabilities are, therefore, appropriate for the Avoidance and Verbal Interaction indices only, though even here the heterogeneity of the items is likely to lead to underestimates of reliability. But the five indices are considerably more homogeneous in content than in form. All indices

143

but one measure the mother's response to an interaction initiated by the child, the exception being the Uses of Toys schedule which does not entail overt interaction. However, every index is concerned with the mother's orientation towards the child's interaction, whether the child is interacting with someone (the mother) or something (toys).

In order to ascertain how far the indices contribute to one or more general dimensions, a correlation matrix was obtained and factor analysed:([2])

	Avoidance	Verbal interaction	Punishment	Reasoning	Toys
Avoidance	1.000				
Verbal Interaction	.284	1.000			
Punishment	.222	.334	1.000		
Reasoning	.233	.150	.262	1.000	
Toys	.374	.318	.214	.213	1.000

Latent Roots	Index	Communality	Factor 1	St. Dev	FL/St.Dev	Final Weight
1. 2.05	Avoidance	.456	.675	1.96	.344	4
2. .88	Verbal interaction	.444	.666	2.74	.242	3
3. .84	Punishment	.395	.629	2.41	.260	3
4. .63	Reasoning	.292	.540	1.24	.434	5
5. .60	Toys	.464	.680	2.38	.286	3

The latent roots indicate that the matrix contains one dominant factor, accounting for .410 of the variance, and the factor loadings demonstrate that it is a general factor. It is of considerable interest to note that the Toys Index, the scoring of which generated the greatest dissatisfaction, has the highest factor loading.

Factor theory states that total variance may be partitioned into variance due to one or more factors (communality), specific variance, and error variance. A reliability coefficient expresses the proportion of variance which is not error. As the communality in this instance is merely the square of the first factor loading, the differences between communality and reliability must represent all the 'true' variance not accounted for by the first factor, i.e. all variance accounted for by subsequent factors plus specific variance. Split-half reliability coefficients were only calculable for the Avoidance and Chatter indices, so the communality-reliability juxtaposition must be limited to these:

	Communality	*Reliability*
Avoidance	.456	.430
Chatter	.444	.466

144

For all practical purposes, then, the communality of either index is equal to its reliability. If the reliability coefficients represent unbiased estimates, then the 'true' variance in each index is completely accounted for by the general factor. The amount by which the reliability coefficients are underestimated — suspected in principle because of the heterogeneity of the items — represents the amount of variance attributable to additional factors plus specific variance, but the underestimation must be truly substantial if additional factor(s) or a specific component are to assume any importance.

As it stands, however, the empirical indications are that the General Factor dominates the non-error variance in those indices where non-error variance is calculable. Accordingly, a General Index has been constructed ($\bar{x}$ = 111, s = 23.6), final approximate weights being derived from dividing the index standard deviations into the index factor loadings. In order to make a more explicit statement about the content of the General Index, a tabular presentation of the individual index-contents is instructive:

Mother is disposed towards:

Situation	*Low Score*	*High Score*
Child asks a difficult question	Evasion	Cognitive Verbal Interaction
Child Talks	Constraint	Verbal Interaction
Child misbehaves (punishment)	Constraint	Absence of constraint
Child misbehaves (Child-oriented reasoning)	Absense of Cognitive Verbal Interaction	Cognitive Verbal Interaction
Uses of Toys	(Instrumental) Mother-Orientation	Cognitive Child-Orientation

A mother with a high score on the Index of Communication and Control is disposed to speak frequently with her child, to promote occasions in which speech is appropriate, to elaborate verbally reasons and rules, and she is concerned to develop her child's active understanding. A mother with a Low Index score is more disposed to limit or discourage verbal interaction, to use physical coercion with her child, and to place a weaker emphasis on language in the moral and cognitive aspects of socialisation.

An Alternative Index

Misgivings about the scaling of items has been one persistent theme in building the separate indices from the schedules. Our faith in the general

145

index could be shaken by the possible unsoundness of the basic foundations on which it was built. Consequently, it was decided to construct parallel indices from dichotomised items, each item being given the same weight as before.

In Schedule E, items 1, 2 and 5 were split 'Never' against 'Sometimes' plus 'Often'; items 3 and 4 'Often' against 'Sometimes' plus 'Never'. Schedule F items were split 'Tell them to stop' plus 'Tell them to wait' against 'Talk to them quickly' plus 'Chat with them'. All Control Schedule items were simply scored on whether the strategy in question had or had not been suggested in any of the nine situations. Finally, the Toys Index from Schedule D was rescored as whether C was first or not, plus whether D (ignoring F) was last or not, plus whether F (ignoring D) was last or not.

A comparison between the original and parallel indices may initially be made in those instances where split-half reliability is calculable:-

	original rxx	*parallel rxx*
Avoidance Index (Schedule F)	.430	293
Verbal Interaction Index (Schedule F)	.466	.295

Thus the reliability of both indices appears to drop very substantially when the constituent items are dichotomised.

As before the five parallel indices were correlated and factor analysed[2]. The latent roots derived from the original and parallel matrices may be compared:-

	Original Latent Roots	*Parallel Latent Roots*
1	2.05	1.87
2	.88	.93
3	.84	.84
4	.63	.72
5	.60	.64

The parallel latent root structure clearly reflects the original, with one dominant factor account for .374 of the matrix variance, but the dominance is not quite so great, for the difference between the variance accounted for by the first and second factors is now less clear. The tendency is reflected in the two sets of communalities:-

146

Index	Original Communality	Parallel Communality
Avoidance	.456	.445
Verbal Interaction	.444	.378
Punishment	.395	.287
Reasoning	.292	.356
Toys	.463	.405

Only the communality of the Child-Oriented Reasoning Index has risen; the remainder have fallen, and except for Avoidance they have fallen quite substantially. It should be added that the communalities of the parallel Avoidance and Verbal Interaction indices are distinctly greater than their reliabilities. This certainly suggests that the parallel reliability coefficients are biased down-wards, but whether additional bias has been picked up in the process of dishotomising must remain uncertain.

Since the parallel form of index-construction effects the index variances differentially, approximate final weights for a parallel General Index were obtained without reference to the original weights:-

Parallel Index	Factor Loading	St. Dev.	FL/St. Dev.	Final Weight
Avoidance	.667	1.491	.447	4
Verbal Interaction	.615	1.136	.541	5
Punishment	.536	1.259	.426	4
Reasoning	.597	.892	.670	6
Toys	.636	1.024	.622	6

The parallel General Index of Mother's Orientation towards Communication and Control was accordingly constructed. ($\bar{x} = 54.2$, $s = 17.3$). Despite the different scoring of the initial items and the different final weight given to the indices, the correlation between the original and the parallel General Index is .941, so that barely over 10% of the variance is specific to the scoring of each Index.

One final comparison can be made. As split-half reliabilities could not be calculated for three of the five indices either in their original or their parallel forms, 'item' split-half reliabilities cannot be calculated for either General Index. However, it is possible to calculate 'index' split halves since the indices are independent of each other, but always with the proviso that in the battle of between-index heterogeneity and correlated time-specific error, the former is likely to win, and so the split-half method is likely to underestimate reliability. However, as there is no discernible reason why there should be any appreciable difference in the relative magnitude of the net bias between the Original and Parallel Indices, the two reliabilities, though probably underestimated, should at least be comparable.

The split-halves decided as most appropriate were Avoidance plus Punishment against Toys plus Chatter plus Reasoning. The final reliabilities were calculated through the Brown-Spearman formula, taking into account the difference in variance between the halves:

Original General Index	Parallel General Index
rxx = .673	rxx = .613

Thus, despite the high correlation between the two General Indices, the reliability of the parallel General Index appears to be clearly reduced.

The high correlation between the two General Indices certainly suggests that one could easily be substituted for the other. However, if a choice has to be made, the weight of evidence is unambiguously on the side of the Original Index. Where it is possible to estimate reliability, the parallel constituent indices appear to be less reliable; the parallel factor structure is less clear, with the general factor less dominant and the communalities generally lower; and finally the reliability of the parallel General Index appears to be lower. Thus on counts both of validity and reliability, the scoring of the Original General Index appears to be superior to that of the parallel General Index.

Notes

(1) Bernstein, B. and Young, D. (1966) 'Some aspects of the relationship between communication and performance in tests' in *Genetic and Environmental Factors in Human Ability* (Eds.) Meade, J. E. and Parkes, A. S. Oliver and Boyd Ltd.

(2) Again using Hendrikson-White factor analysis program on the IBM 7090 at Imperial College. The varimax rotation to an oblique solution, and the higher order factors options have been used where possible. See Appendix I, note (4).

THE RELATIONSHIP BETWEEN SOCIAL CLASS AND MOTHER'S ORIENTATION TOWARDS COMMUNICATION AND CONTROL

by W. Brandis

The matrix of correlations between the two sets of indices for the overall sample is as follows:-

$r(n = 351)$		Mother's Orientation:	
		Index I	Index II
	Index I	.571	.563
Social Class :			
	Index II	.576	.568

No matter how either Index is scored, the correlation between social class and mother's orientation towards communication and control is consistently high at between .56 and .58.

But the 'sample' is in no sense randomly selected from any definable population. It consists of the new intake in each of 10 primary schools selected from a working-class area (contributing 204 mothers), and 5 primary schools selected from a middle-class area (contributing 147 mothers). In order to determine whether the magnitude of the relationship is in any sense a function of the sampling procedure, the correlations presented above have been partitioned into their between-area and within-area components, and the individual area relationships have in turn been partitioned into their between-schools and within-schools components. Taking mother's orientation as the criterion variable, a series of tests for homogeneity of regression (interaction) have been performed within a nested analysis of covariance design.

Within each area, the individual within-schools regressions do not differ significantly from each other in any of the four relationships, and therefore may be combined into pooled within-schools regression coefficients. Furthermore, there are no significant differences between the pooled within-schools and between-schools regressions (nor is there any evidence of departure from linearity in the between-schools regressions), so that it is permissible to represent each relationship in each area by the appropriate total area regression coefficient. In the overall sample, however, while the respective pooled within-areas and the between-areas

149

regressions also do not differ significantly from each other, one powerful interaction does appear throughout. The regression coefficients in the working-class area are consistently higher than those in the middle-class area:

FI,347:   *Y = Mother's Orientation:*
                                            Index I   *Index II*

                        Index I   5.92p < .05   4.64p < .05

X = Social Class:

                        Index II   4.17p < .05   3.25 not sig.

At this point, a comparison between the Area variances for each of the four indices is illuminating:

Total Variance	*Social Class*		*Mother's Orientation*	
	Index I	*Index II*	*Index I*	*Index II*
W.C. Area (df = 203)	2.06	4.58	539	252
M.C. Area (df = 146)	3.17	5.41	308	206
Chi-squared (df = 1)	7.41	1.37	12.40	2.07
	p < .01	not sig.	p < .001	not sig.

The mother's orientation variance is greater in the working class than in the middle-class area, and for the more reliable Index I this difference is significant. On the other hand, the social class variance is greater in the middle-class than in the working-class area, so that the regression coefficients in the former should be relatively greater and the significance of difference between areas smaller than if the two social class variances had been equal. Since this inequality is largely a function of unequal between-schools variance, the two social class variances are more nearly standardised by substituting the pooled within-schools variance for the total variances:

Within-Schools Variance	*Social Class*		*Mother's Orientation*	
	Index I	*Index II*	*Index I*	*Index II*
W.C. Area (df = 194)	1.91	4.31	549	253
M.C. Area (df = 142)	2.49	4.36	289	200
Chi-squared (df = 1)	3.66	0.00	15.94	2.81
	not sig.	not sig.	p < .001	not sig.

Substituting the pooled within-schools for the total Area regression coefficients, the differences between the two Areas are (predictably) sharpened:

$F1,334$ $Y = Mother's\ Orientation$
                                    Index I   *Index II*

              Index I   9.05p < .01   6.08p < .05

$X = Social\ Class:$

              Index II   6.83p < .01   4.44p < .05

Clearly, then social class affects the mother's orientation towards Communication and Control in the working-class area much more dramatically than in the middle-class area, no matter which way either variable is scored. Since the overwhelming distinction between the two areas is their social class composition, and in the absence of any other discernible area-specific characteristics which might explain such differences, it seems reasonable to suggest that the mother's orientation towards Communication and Control clearly differentiates working-class strata, but fails to discriminate very adequately between middle-class strata. Indeed, the relative homogeneity of mother's orientation towards Communication and Control in the middle-class area indicates that its power to discriminate between anything at all within the middle-class is considerably reduced. The implication is that more subtle measures are required to ascertain the stylistic and ideological differences between middle-class strata. It can be argued, then, that middle-class mothers are generally oriented towards a more individuated relationship between child and environment, and that there are critical sub-dimensions within this general orientation which differentiate the social strata in the middle-class.

This kind of speculation is difficult to follow up empirically from the research reported in this paper, particularly since the data do no not readily lend themselves to the extraction of any but the most general factors. A second interview schedule has accordingly been constructed and administered to over 300 mothers from the original samples. This interview schedule has been designed to explore systematically the information obtained in the original interview. It consists almost entirely of closed inventories of logically independent items and so will lend itself readily to a series of factor analyses. Results from the analysis of this new data will be reported in a later monograph in this series.

APPENDIX IV

Disagreement Schedule

On some of these the school sometimes has one idea and the parents another. Could you tick the ones where you think there might be disagreement between school and parents.

	There might be disagreement

*1. What time children go to bed
2. How they behave at school
*3. The television or radio programmes the child sees or hears at home.
4. The clothes children wear at school.
*5 The friends children have.
6. The jobs they might do when they leave school.
7. The age at which they should leave school.
*8. Children's health
9. The books they read.
10. Their progress at school.
11. The subjects they learn.
12. How they get on with teachers.
*13. If they are unfortunate enough to get into trouble with the police.
*14. How they behave at home.
*15. How they get on with their parents.
16. What kind of school they go to when they are eleven.
*17. What is considered right from wrong.
*18. What they are told about sex.
*19. Their manners.
*20. How much money they have to spend.
21. How much the child is punished at school.
22. The amount of homework children should do.

---

*items contributing to index of Disagreements within the Home area.

APPENDIX V

Boundary Schedule

Here is a list of things which you may feel are mainly the school's job, or the parent's, or in which both have an interest. We are not thinking of five year olds, but *children of all ages.* Please tick the column you think is right.

	†Mainly Parents	Both Parents and School	†Mainly School
1. What time children go to bed.			
*2. How they behave at school.			
3. The television or radio programmes the child sees or hears at home.			
*4. The clothes children wear at school.			
5. The friends children have.			
*6. The jobs they might do when they leave school.			
*7. The age at which they should leave school.			
8. Children's health.			
*9. The books they read.			
*10. Their progress at school.			
*11. The subjects they learn.			
*12. How they get on with teachers.			
13. If they are unfortunate enough to get into trouble with the police.			
14. How they behave at home.			
15. How they get on with their parents.			
*16. What kind of school they go to when they are eleven.			
17. What is considered right from wrong.			
18. What they are told about sex.			
19. Their manners.			
20. How much money they have to spend.			
*21. How the child is punished at school.			
*22. The amount of homework children should do.			

* items contributing to index of Boundary with reference to the school area.

† both categories given the same score.